In *The Mission Matrix*, Bendor-Samuel and Franklin have given mission thinker-practitioners a tidy reference volume and toolkit. Don't be fooled by the seemingly small size of this volume – these two TCKs' informed depth of reflection and grass-roots familiarity with the subject is reflected in the skill in which they have weaved together, concisely and creatively, an amazing breadth of mission history, theological perspectives and missiological strategy in a brilliant and refreshingly relevant framework for missional engagement. This is a priceless resource and essential read not just for students of mission but for any believer who wants to follow Christ's Way of mission.

Ivan Satyavrata, PhD, Board Chair, World Vision International

The history of mission, its successes and its downfalls, and the theologies behind mission paradigms are all packed into this priceless little book! The authors are offering a true gift to the church – all the tools necessary for us to form a responsible theology of mission obedient to the life of the Trinity.

Myrto Theocharous, PhD, Professor of Hebrew and Old Testament,
Greek Bible College, Athens, Greece

The Mission Matrix acquaints the reader with Mission Theology and practice of mission. It convincingly seeks not to present a singular mission theology – from the authors or others – but provides a comprehensive guide through the field and the discipline.

Marina Ngursangzeli Behera, Research Tutor, MPhil Stage Leader and Editor of Transformation, *Oxford Centre for Mission Studies*

The Mission Matrix voices a clarion call to rethink our theoretical and practical approaches to mission. Recognizing the myriad mission theologians who reflected on and responded to their over 2000 years of mission history, this book also acknowledges the current and rapidly changing global context of mission and the resulting questions for the church and its mission practitioners. *The Mission Matrix* presents a multidisciplinary path from the centre of our triune God and his word, as we re-evaluate our Mission Theologies and adjust our theories and practice accordingly.

Stephen Coertze, PhD, Executive Director, Wycliffe Global Alliance

This book represents a significant endeavour to provide an accessible introductory handbook of current thinking on Mission Theology.

William Dyrness, (D)Theol, Dean Emeritus and Senior Professor of Theology and Culture, Fuller Theological Seminary

This introductory text offers a well-informed and wide-ranging taster of the riches of theology of mission, from biblical texts to missional readings and Trinitarian approaches. Located as a Protestant mission theology, it is open to learning from the church globally, including different continents and traditions. I can't think of a better start for the reflective practitioner who embraces integrity, creativity, openness, and curiosity in participating in God's mission.

Kirsteen Kim, PhD, Paul E. Pierson Professor of World Christianity and Associate Dean for the Center for Missiological Research, Fuller Theological Seminary, USA

We are living in the season of great changes in mission. A good theology of mission is critical. Old paradigms are not helpful anymore. To create new ones, we need to understand where we have come from and where we are now. This accessible book offers readers an important perspective that helps them discern the times as well as a theological foundation of mission on which they can build. We need more books like this.

Harvey Kwiyani, PhD, CEO of Global Connections, UK

Mind the gaps! In our fragmented world, what tools are needed to identify gaps in our understanding of God's mission? *The Mission Matrix* is a reflective journey through history, paradigms, mission theology, human effort, and partnership with a God of surprises. It invites us to learn from failure, missional hermeneutics, and the global church. Be equipped and inspired to re-examine, re-adjust, and discover new tools for engaging in mission.

Diane Marshall, PhD, Leadership Mentor, former Global Director of
Regional Development, SIM International

The global mission community is sorely in need of a theological schema to help us better navigate a rapidly changing world in partnership with an increasingly diverse global church. Methodologies too quickly become rigid, but a contextually malleable matrix can be powerfully agile. *The Mission Matrix* provides us with exactly that – a context-sensitive tool that should be considered indispensable for every reflective practitioner of mission seeking to strengthen their and others' participation in God's mission.

Jay Mātenga, PhD, Executive Director, Mission Commission,
World Evangelical Alliance

The Mission Matrix provides a highly accessible exploration into mission theology within the contemporary global landscape. Written by two esteemed scholar-practitioners, Paul Bendor-Samuel and Kirk Franklin trace the development of mission theology throughout church history. They then highlight the significance of mission theology for our dynamic and increasingly complex global world. This volume offers a wonderful primer on contemporary missiology.

Gregg A. Okesson, PhD, Author of A Public Missiology: How Local
Churches Witness to a Complex World, *Asbury Theological Seminary*

Theology, even more so, Mission Theology, cannot be an ivory tower enterprise and neither can mission practice proceed without it being anchored in solid theological reflection. In this introductory, really packed book, Franklin and Bendor-Samuel succeed in demonstrating how Mission Theology and mission practice belong inseparably together. This work should help to cement cooperation between mission theologians and practitioners. It has much to offer to the academy as well as the church.

Rev. Prof. B. Y. Quarshie, Rector, Akrofi-Christaller Institute of Theology,
Mission and Culture, Ghana

The Mission Matrix

Mission Theologies for
Diverse Mission Landscapes

Series Preface

Regnum Studies in Mission are born from the lived experience of Christians and Christian communities in mission, especially but not solely in the fast growing churches among the poor of the world. These churches have more to tell than stories of growth. They are making significant impacts on their cultures in the cause of Christ. They are producing 'cultural products' which express the reality of Christian faith, hope and love in their societies.

Regnum Studies in Mission are the fruit often of rigorous research to the highest international standards and always of authentic Christian engagement in the transformation of people and societies. And these are for the world. The formation of Christian theology, missiology and practice in the twenty-first century will depend to a great extent on the active participation of growing churches contributing biblical and culturally appropriate expressions of Christian practice to inform World Christianity.

Series Editors

The Mission Matrix

Mission Theologies for Diverse Mission Landscapes

by

Kirk Franklin and Paul Bendor-Samuel, with Deborah Crough

First published 2024 by Regnum Books International

Regnum is an imprint of the Oxford Centre for Mission Studies
St. Philip and St. James Church
Woodstock Road
Oxford, OX2 6HR, UK
www.regnumbooks.net

British Library Cataloguing in Publication Data
A catalogue record for this book is available from the British Library

ISBN: 979-8-8898-3897-5
eBook ISBN: 979-8-8898-3898-2

Typeset by Words by Design

Distributed by Fortress Press in the US, Canada, India, and Brazil

Contents

Abbreviations

AACC	All Africa Conference of Churches
BAM	Business as Mission
CMS	Church Missionary Society
COMIBAM	Cooperación Misionera Iberoamericana
CWME	Commission on World Mission and Evangelism
FBO	Faith-Based Organisation
IMC	International Mission Council
LCWE	Lausanne Congress on Worldwide Evangelization
LMS	London Missionary Society
MAF	Mission Aviation Fellowship
NGO	Non-Governmental Organisation
OCMS	Oxford Centre for Mission Studies
TCK	Third Culture Kid
UBS	United Bible Societies
UUPG	Unengaged, Unreached People Groups
WCC	World Council of Churches
WWI	World War I
WWII	World War II

Introduction

There are many books on Mission Theology, and this one focuses on the connection between theology and practice in rapidly changing mission contexts. *The Mission Matrix* probes the extensive realm of Mission Theology, dissecting its terminology and discerning its profound implications regarding God's mission (*missio Dei*) primarily from the vantage point of the Protestant mission movement. In the following pages, we embark on a concise journey of mission history and the ever-evolving landscape of contemporary mission contexts. We aim to equip you with the tools necessary to apply Mission Theology's frameworks to intricate issues and diverse situations and to strengthen your ability to interpret and implement missiological critical thinking and reflection within your specific field of ministry.

Through this endeavour, we aspire to facilitate your growth as a reflective practitioner, fostering qualities such as integrity, creativity, openness, and curiosity within the realm of mission. We invite you to embark on a personal exploration, a journey that enables you to scrutinise the factors that have shaped your own Mission Theology. This reflective process, conducted against the backdrop of your engagement with Scripture, unique context, ministry experiences, and personal insights, promises to be a transformative experience. Our ultimate aspiration is that this book not only equips and informs but also ignites a passion within you – an insatiable hunger to delve deeper into the profound world of God's mission through Mission Theology. We hope these pages leave you yearning for a continued pursuit of knowledge and wisdom in the realm of mission.

The origins of this book formed with our work with PhD students who needed a foundation of Mission Theology in their orientation program at the Oxford Centre for Mission Studies (OCMS). Paul started teaching the content in early 2021. In 2022, we began drawing from this material for another OCMS programme, the Integrated Mission Leader's professional development course for international mission agency leaders. Simultaneously, Kirk used some of the material in courses he developed and taught at Melbourne School of Theology's Master of Missional Leadership. As we engaged with participants of these programmes and heard their positive responses, we became convinced of the need for a book that could serve both mission and church leaders and practitioners.

Our backgrounds shaped our approach to Mission Theology because we're both Third Culture Kids (TCKs). Our parents served with Wycliffe Bible Translators and SIL International. We didn't meet each other in childhood, but rather as mission leaders in 2008 when Paul was the International Director of Interserve and Kirk was the Executive Director of Wycliffe Global Alliance.

Kirk was born and raised in Papua New Guinea and served there in his early years in mission agency media communications, then later in Australia and globally as a mission executive. During the past decade, he pursued several academic degrees in missiology. Kirk's interests include teaching in missiology, missional leadership development, global leadership topics, mentoring ministry leaders, and local church ministry.

Paul's professional training in family medicine and public health fostered a spirit of enquiry and reflective practice. He and his family served for 12 years in Tunisia, leading a development organisation, and then 12 years leading Interserve, an interdenominational, international mission agency focused on Asia and the Middle East. His interests include Christian organisational spirituality and development, the changing cross-cultural mission paradigm, mission as discipleship, and leadership development.

Together, Paul and Kirk approach Mission Theology neither as an abstract subject nor from a purely academic perspective but through the lens of lived experiences. We both would have liked to have had a book like this when we were starting and serving in our various mission roles to help equip us on our missional journey.

As you read this book, you will see how mission is a slippery word with many meanings. At the same time, within the Protestant evangelical and Pentecostal worlds, ideas and assumptions about mission remain profoundly shaped by the cross-cultural movement that arose in the late eighteenth century and flourished in the nineteenth and twentieth centuries. That God has chosen to use this understanding and practice of mission, with all its messiness, is cause for thanksgiving and worship. The church, today, serves in a very different world than that of missionary envoys like William Carey, Hudson Taylor, and Cameron Townsend. And the church itself has been transformed.

This radical transformation of the church into a global reality, rooted in countless different contexts, sparkling with linguistic, cultural, and theological diversity, demands we re-examine what faithful witness and participation in God's ultimate purposes look like today. We recognise the complexities and challenges of global issues such as inequality, climate change, rising nationalism, political and economic instability, mass movement of peoples, artificial intelligence, and more. While all contextual realities demand critical mission theological reflection and practical engagement, the most significant factor driving our concern for new mission theological reflection is the changing demographics and diversity of the global church. This book attempts to help us, as mission thinkers and practitioners, develop the essential theological tools to enable us to participate more fully and faithfully in God's life-giving, renewing, and reconciling mission.

A word about the book title's use of 'matrix': we found a journal article by Richard Bliese about a 'mission matrix' that consisted of 'a grid of ecclesiological categories, driven by a theology of mission' as a system for 'pastoral praxis of mission'.[1] While we don't use his grid, we do see the value of describing Mission Theology as a matrix because it 'constitutes the place or point from which something else originates, takes form, or develops'.[2] That is what our mission matrix attempts to achieve as we navigate the Mission Theology landscapes formed and forming as we participate in God's mission.[3] This is the iterative, cyclical nature of how we wrote the book – we introduce a theme, then revisit it or look at it from a different angle. This is how Mission Theology is developed – constantly revisiting assumptions, contexts, and lived experiences.

Each chapter ends with reflective questions to help you contemplate the impact of the material and to give a starting point to connect what we've written with your own experience. That's where the real growth will take place. We provide a bibliography for those who want to read further.

Finally, we are thankful for Deborah Crough's role as our editor. She and her late husband, Dave, worked with Kirk on his first book, *Towards Global Missional Leadership* (2017), and she worked with Susan Van Wynen and Kirk on *A Missional Leadership History* (2022). We're also grateful to Susan for her editorial suggestions, which have improved our work. In addition, our thanks go to Marina Behera and Stephen Coertze for their editorial suggestions, and to William Dyrness, who carefully advised on a restructuring of our work.

---

[1] Richard Bliese, "The Mission Matrix: Mapping Out the Complexities of a Missional Ecclesiology," *Word & World* 26, no. 3 (2006): 238.

[2] "Matrix," accessed 5 June 2023, from https://www.dictionary.com/browse/matrix.

[3] In researching a title, we asked ChatGPT for its recommendation based on the purpose of this book. It suggested 'Mission Matrix: Navigating the Theological Landscape of Today's Mission Journey.'

PART ONE

MISSION LANDSCAPES

1. Revealing the Divine Initiative

Introduction

This chapter examines the concept of *missio Dei*, or the mission of God, and its influence on our understanding of Christian mission. The theology of mission has unfolded over centuries, and the relevance of *missio Dei* has come to the fore relatively recently. To illustrate, early church father St Augustine (354–430 CE) is credited with using the term *missio Dei* to describe 'God's work in which the church and the faithful participate'.[1] That said, there is no evidence that St Augustine or the early church fathers used the term in relation to mission as we have come to understand it. In the sixteenth century, Gisbertus Voetius described mission as flowing from the heart of God. In 1991, David Bosch observed how *missio Dei* was associated with the doctrine of the Trinity dating back to the sixteenth century. From 1952 onward, the idea of the *missio Dei* became a more common phrase in theology, initially in ecumenical circles and within the past 25 years in evangelicalism.[2]

Our understanding of God's mission exists in evolving circumstances, and though God does not change, context does, altering how we think about and participate in his mission. Various constructions, frameworks, and applications through theological grids create an ongoing challenge when interpreting the *missio Dei*. This, in turn, makes *missio Dei* an 'elastic concept'[3] as we are continuously presented with issues to reconsider and then integrate, bringing more implications to our practice. For example, in recent years, creation care has become a concern for mission. Increasing awareness of the destruction of the natural environment affected by our economic models and behaviour adjusts as we learn more about God's redemptive intentions in and for our world.

To better understand the development of the *missio Dei*, we benefit from exploring the following key markers in recent history.

Mission as Western Conquest (1800s–1910)

Andrew Walls sees the spiritual motivation of God's people through two simultaneous impulses or approaches to mission that contributed to the expansion of the Christian faith in the nineteenth century:

(1) With the 'crusading mode', some missionaries inadvertently aligned themselves with colonial Christendom governments. They used military language to describe their actions and compared God's mission to a conquest that expanded their territory. Christian mission was about occupying new ground

---

[1] Thomas Kemper, "The *Missio Dei* in Contemporary Context," *International Bulletin of Missionary Research* 38, no. 4 (2014): 188.

[2] Kemper, 188.

[3] Gary Tyra, *A Missional Orthodoxy: Theology and Ministry in a Post-Christian Context* (Downers Grove: IVP Academic, 2013), 310.

for Christ because some parts of the world were Christian while others were not. Woven into this was the assumption that Christianity, as practised in the West, produced a superior culture. Therefore, the need to Christianise entire people groups was implicit within the gospel. Michael Stroope writes, 'Representatives of mission conquered, coerced, and destroyed [local cultures] in the name of Christianity.'[4] Such 'colonial mission' meant people from the US and England were sent overseas, which was patterned on earlier Spanish and Dutch mission efforts. Even in the crusading mode, missionaries sought to do good by bringing Western medical attention where it was needed. Another form of expansion was Western education, whether in English or the local vernacular.

(2) The 'missionary mode' could describe situations where Christian missionaries sincerely and truthfully sought to proclaim the gospel and seek out new followers to disciple in their faith.[5] For example, Robert Woodberry discovered that in locations significantly served by Protestant missionaries in the past, they 'are on average more economically developed today, with comparatively better health, lower infant mortality, lower corruption, greater literacy, higher educational attainment (especially for women), and more robust membership in nongovernmental associations'.[6]

Andrew Kirk uses another comparison, interweaving both crusade and manifest destiny (the belief that God entrusted a chosen nation with the responsibility of making the world better), likening the missionary initiative to a business persuasively selling Christianity, packaged in the form of European civilisation and the gospel.[7]

At the Edinburgh World Missionary Conference of 1910, Robert E. Speer promoted the concept of mission as 'conquest'.[8] At the close of the conference, chairman John R. Mott boldly proclaimed that conquest to the ends of the earth would result in evangelising the world in our generation. A focused effort towards world mission to the ends of the earth had begun. It should be noted that Mott was not necessarily trying to present a victorious perspective of mission, as he was in fact known for his ecumenicalism and cross-cultural relationships.

The slogan 'evangelisation of the world in our generation' represented this moment of confident Christianity, following a century of Christian expansion, when Christianity peaked at approximately 34% of the world's population self-identifying as Christian. It has never surpassed that number since. Thousands of Westerners once claimed to be 'Christian' (as did others who were influenced) merely to distinguish themselves from being 'heathen' or belonging to another major world religion. To be Western was to be 'Christian', whether or not they

---

[4] Michael Stroope, *Transcending Mission: The Eclipse of a Modern Tradition* (London: Apollos, 2017), xiv.

[5] Andrew Walls, "Afterword: Christian Mission in a Five-Hundred-Year Context," in *Mission in the 21st Century*, ed. Andrew Walls and Cathy Ross (Maryknoll: Orbis Books, 2008), 196.

[6] Andrea Palpant Dilley, "The World the Missionaries Made," *Christianity Today*, 2014.

[7] Andrew Kirk, *What Is Mission?* (Minneapolis: Fortress Press, 2000), 23.

[8] Mark Noll, *Turning Points: Decisive Moments in the History of Christianity*, 3rd ed. (Grand Rapids: Baker Academic, 2012), 262.

had the slightest connection with actual Christianity. Gina Zurlo states that this is comprised of 'four major Christian traditions: (1) Catholics, (2) Orthodox (both Eastern and Oriental), (3) Protestants (including Anglicans), and (4) Independents' – 'churches or movements that self-identify as Christian but are independent of historic Christianity' and are comprised of churches and denominations that don't define themselves by the first three categories.[9]

During the great church and missionary expansion of the late nineteenth and early twentieth centuries, Christians of this era seemed confident that the purpose and endeavour of mission would somehow be complete. Mott logically believed that all available Christian resources would be quickly deployed to support this advance. Those present at the conference would be responsible for initiating a comprehensive plan for evangelisation that would see the world fully 'reached' in the foreseeable future.[10]

Such examples gave missiologists like David Bosch a reason to see a 'clear and substantial connection between the expansion of the European colonial powers and the advance of the church', or what we call 'the modern, Enlightenment paradigm of mission'.[11] Consequently, mission vocabulary associated with the *missio Dei* became historically and indistinguishably linked with the colonial era and was commissioned by its royal powers.[12]

Within four short years of the Edinburgh event, the incredible air of optimism and confidence was quickly disrupted by major worldwide happenings, including World War I (1914–1918), the Great Influenza (Spanish flu) pandemic (1918), the Great Depression (1929–1933), and World War II (1939–1945). In World War I, for example, European Christian nations were destroying each other in a conflict that lasted four years and cost over nine million military and 13 million civilian lives (including six million lost to famine and disease) and another 23 million wounded. Coupled with World War II, this devastated confidence in the gospel and challenged optimistic mission rhetoric.

Mission was shaped by four factors that emerged from this era:

1. The collapse of the European empires meant a significant loss of influence through colonialism.

2. The over-confidence arising from the Enlightenment was ill-founded, presuming that humanity could 'change the world'.[13]

3. Western Christian leaders realised that the church was growing more rapidly outside of the West than it was in Europe and North America.

---

[9] Gina Zurlo, *Global Christianity: A Guide to the World's Largest Religion from Afghanistan to Zimbabwe* (Grand Rapids: Zondervan Academic, 2022), xvii–xviii.
[10] Noll, 264.
[11] Stroope, xvi.
[12] Stroope, xvii.
[13] Keith Whitfield, "The Triune God: The God of Mission," in *Theology and Practice of Mission: God, the Church, and the Nations*, ed. Bruce R. Ashford (Nashville: B & H Publishing Group, 2011), 18.

4. A humbler approach to mission was characterised as realising the depravity of the sinful human condition and its separation from God.[14]

Tensions in Mission Theology (1928–1950)

During the last century, the understanding of mission and Mission Theology developed through a series of gatherings called World Missionary Conferences organised by the International Mission Council (IMC). These were attended by key leaders of mission that sought to pick up where Edinburgh 1910 left off. We can trace the evolution of thinking about the *missio Dei* and Mission Theology through the IMC conferences.

At the 1928 World Missionary Conference in Jerusalem, differences of opinion arose between those who thought *missio Dei* was exclusively about evangelism through proclamation and those who saw mission as focused on the social implications of the gospel. We see the beginnings of tension within the worldwide mission movement around this very soon after WWII.

In the 1932 conference at Brandenburg, Germany, theologian Karl Barth introduced Protestant reflections on mission as the 'activity of God'. Mission acts as 'a witness' to the world and all humanity of the action and activity of God[15] and depends entirely on Christ's grace, arising from the heart of the triune God. The church is missionary, empowered by the Holy Spirit, participating in God's mission with the focus now on all creation. Barth influenced a wider circle of theological development concerning where mission was centred – it originated as God's activity rather than the human activity of the church – and changed the understanding of where ownership of mission resides – shifting it from the church to God. Through Barth, the 'language of *missio Dei* reframed mission activity initiated and sustained by God, and thus it created... a measure of distinction and sacredness for mission',[16] sacred because mission is the overflow of God's love.

Further theological tensions surfaced concerning how Christian mission related to other world religions at the 1938 conference in Tambaram, India. W.E. Hocking questioned the lack of cooperation between Christians and followers of other religions, whom he saw as allies against the mutual enemy of secularism. On the other hand, Hendrick Kramer emphasised mission as primarily the proclamation of the gospel. Ultimately, we see the same tensions today as could be seen emerging in the 1930s.

Post-WWII, at the conference in 1947 in Whitby, Canada, a mood of submission to God as humble partners in mission existed. After the war, the world was healing from deep divisions and the 112 participants who came to the conference focused on evaluating how mission efforts were affected adversely

---

[14] Kirsteen Kim, *Joining in With the Spirit: Connecting World Church and Local Mission* (London: Epworth, 2009), 23.

[15] Francis Anekwe Oborji, *Concepts of Mission: The Evolution of Contemporary Missiology* (Maryknoll: Orbis Books, 2006), 134.

[16] Stroope, xv.

by the war. Discussions about representing the 'witness of the church' occurred, along with how to demonstrate mission partnership.[17] There were two issues in focus:

1. 'Joint service in mission between former enemies who now met each other… for the first time after the war' and how they would now engage
2. 'Mission societies from the North serving together with the young independent churches from the [global] South.' Therefore, the significance of this conference was how it gave 'a theological handle that captured the nature of this relationship, namely the motto "partnership in obedience"'.[18]

These IMC-organised conferences began to highlight issues in mission that are still with us today. Importantly, the concept of mission initiated by and belonging to God started to take centre stage.

Missio Dei's Theological Development (1950–1965)

At the World Missionary Conference in 1952 in Willingen, Germany, Karl Hartenstein built on Barth's influence, which points to mission as the 'labour of the triune God [because]… mission is an attribute of God',[19] originating in and flowing from his nature. Hartenstein stated that mission occurred within the triune God's overall plan for salvation because 'God is mission'.[20] At the conference, the term *missio Dei* emerged and became widely used within the church, including in Protestant, evangelical, and Roman Catholic movements. Hartenstein positioned mission 'as the cause of the Trinitarian God' rather than merely the responsibility of the church, representing a profound shift.[21] Though Barth introduced the concept, only now was it gaining momentum. Rather than mission originating from the church or being church-centred, it flows from the heart of God, who initiates mission and empowers the church to go into the whole world with the whole gospel. Francis Oborji states that 'the church exists because there is *missio Dei*'.[22] However, the church's role is not marginalised in mission, even though God's mission is greater than the missionary actions of the church itself. The church's role is to be 'an instrument of mission… in the movement of God's love' for all humanity.[23]

After Willingen, *missio Dei* was mentioned in the writings and speaking of mission leaders but was not used widely until 1958 when Georg Vicedom released his book *The Mission of God* (in German, with an English translation in 1964), which had a significant impact on the mission world. Vicedom brought greater clarity to the relationship between mission and the Trinity by presenting

---

[17] Henning Wrogemann, *Theologies of Mission*, trans. Karl E. Bohmer, *Intercultural Theology Vol. 2* (Downers Grove: IVP Academic, 2018), 64.

[18] Wrogemann, 64.

[19] Oborji, 134.

[20] Stephen Bevans, and Roger Schroeder, *Constants in Context: A Theology for Mission Today* (Maryknoll: Orbis Books, 2004), 57.

[21] Oborji, 134.

[22] Oborji, 135.

[23] Oborji, 135.

the triune God as the model for mission, influencing both spirit and action or activity. God's loving will and nature provide the origin and basis for mission, with the church as the instrument for mission.

The IMC was renamed the Commission on World Mission and Evangelism (CWME) when IMC merged with the World Council of Churches (WCC) in 1961. At CWME's conference in 1963 in Mexico City, mission and evangelism were brought together. They had previously been separated by forces pulling them towards either the social justice issues or the proclamation side of mission. Mission was no longer primarily a one-directional action from the well-known slogan the 'West to the rest', but was occurring in all directions. In 1963, those in the Protestant missionary movement were only beginning to understand that mission was no longer limited to the church's sending of cross-cultural missionaries overseas and no longer based primarily on geography. Instead, mission was founded on the 'belief, conviction, and commitment' of all the church was sent to do.[24] It was the church responding to God's call.

Missio Dei's Widening Influence (1966–1990)

Theologian J.C. Hoekendijk understood *missio Dei* to be based on 'God's self-revelation as the One who loves the world'.[25] God's action is in and with the world, and he invites the church to participate through specific methods, 'times and places, or in response to particular needs'.[26] The church's role in mission was limited to 'a function of God's work for worldly *shalom*'.[27] The church was being secularised and stripped of its transcendent purpose.[28]

While Hoekendijk's position gained popularity, others saw the church's role in the *missio Dei* not in a secular sense but as the principal channel by which God's redemption occurs in the world. This idea that God's work in the world is more significant than his work in the church opened the notion of how God could be at work outside the church, including through other religions, and raised the question of whether and how the church could participate in that work through other faiths.

The CWME began to draw together a wider group, which was seen at the 1989 San Antonio Conference on World Mission and Evangelism. There was some acceptance of *missio Dei* by some evangelicals beyond mainline Protestants, Eastern Orthodox, and Roman Catholics.

By now, Lesslie Newbigin's emphasis on the role of the triune God in mission became prominent. Newbigin stated that since God is the overall ruler, the church is called to boldly proclaim the kingdom of God as being 'over all

---

[24] Kirk, 24.

[25] Oborji, 144.

[26] Oborji, 144.

[27] Oborji, 144.

[28] David Bosch, *Transforming Mission: Paradigm Shifts in Theology of Mission* (Maryknoll: Orbis Books, 1991), 326.

things'.[29] According to Newbigin, this means all members of the Trinity are involved in God's mission: the Father proclaims the kingdom, the Son offers new life, and the Holy Spirit bears witness to the activity of the triune God, through whom the church has 'missional authority' to proclaim and demonstrate the gospel.[30] The issue of authority is significant. Under Christendom's influence, biblical Trinitarian authority for mission was 'replaced by a cultural, institutional, or pragmatic one', and with the 'collapse of Christendom', such authority is now 'utterly discredited'.[31] Newbigin's call for a Trinitarian missiology was an insightful call to return to the authority of the triune God in mission rather than the assumed authority of Christendom's church.

David Bosch and *Missio Dei*

Theologian David Bosch's work refining the understanding of *missio Dei* is critical and of lasting significance. His *Transforming Mission* continues to be extensively cited on the topic. Bosch differentiates mission dimensionally and intentionally. As dimensional, mission's nature is theological, historical, and eschatological.[32] As intentional, mission 'has direct involvement in society… such as evangelism and work for justice and peace'.[33]

Bosch observed how *missio Dei* had been interpreted through mission history in several ways:

1. In soteriological terms, 'saving individuals from eternal damnation'.
2. In cultural terms, bringing the so-called 'blessings of the Christian West' to people from the Global South and East.
3. In ecclesiastical terms, the physical growth of the church or a denomination.
4. Regarding salvation history, the world 'would be transformed into the kingdom of God'.[34]

Different times in history, and various components of the church, emphasise the range of characteristics of those four perspectives of the *missio Dei*.

For Bosch, the *missio Dei* and the church's role in mission are tied together by the church's call to reflect the triune God. Bosch stated that mission originates only from the heart of the triune God as the 'deepest source of mission'.[35] The church is missionary because it exists to be sent for God's mission. Almost as a warning, Bosch states that the church can only be missionary if it is out in the

---

[29] Lesslie Newbigin, *The Open Secret: An Introduction to the Theology of Mission*, revised edition (Grand Rapids: Wm B. Eerdmans, 1995), 29.
[30] Timothy Tennent, *Invitation to World Missions: A Trinitarian Missiology of the Twenty-First Century* (Grand Rapids: Kregel Academic & Professional, 2010), 67.
[31] Tennent, 67.
[32] Bosch, 498.
[33] Bosch, 373.
[34] Bosch, 389.
[35] Bevans, and Schroeder, 303.

world as a 'sent community'[36] and acting differently from the world as a prophetic 'contrast community'.[37] The end result of God's mission will be a state of *shalom* when God's 'universal reconciliation and peace' will reign over all.[38]

Evangelicalism

The Lausanne Committee for World Evangelization (LCWE) met in 1974 (called Lausanne I). An intense ideological discussion occurred, centred between Western voices and theologians and Christians from the Majority World. The context was how 'ultra-liberal definitions of mission in the early part of the twentieth century… emphasized social justice at the expense of evangelization'.[39] Those from the West focused on mission as proclamation, and those from the Majority World interpreted God's mission as the wholeness of God's activity in the world, bringing about the transformation of unjust structures and institutionalised sin, as well as the personal salvation of those who confessed Jesus as Lord. Therefore, the ensuing debate corrected a 'shortsightedness among evangelicals'[40] concerning the social justice–evangelism dynamic. The result in the *Lausanne Covenant* posited 'social concern [as] an integral place in theology and practice of mission, albeit in varying degrees'.[41]

The *Lausanne Covenant* recognised that the universal church – as a community rather than an institution – is at the centre of God's mission and is his means of proclaiming the gospel. Later, the Lausanne Theological Working Group described 'the whole church', identifying it with the Nicene Creed as 'one, holy, catholic, and apostolic church'.[42] This 'creedal formulation' became Lausanne's understanding of involvement in the *missio Dei*.[43]

Later, Lausanne's *Manila Manifesto* (1989) stated that mission encompasses the 'whole gospel' that establishes the kingdom of God on earth through his 'liberating plan' for his redeemed community.[44]

LCWE became the Lausanne Movement, and its 2010 *Cape Town Commitment* intentionally builds on the earlier *Covenant*, broadening its

---

[36] Stanley Skreslet, *Comprehending Mission: The Questions, Methods, Themes, Problems and Prospects of Missiology* (Maryknoll: Orbis Books, 2012), 32.

[37] Heleen Zorgdrager, "Moral Guardian or Kenotic Servant? A Theological View of the Role of Churches in Empowering Civil Society in Ukraine," *Occasional Papers on Religion in Eastern Europe* 32, no. 4 (2012): 27.

[38] Oborji, 134.

[39] Al Tizon, *Transformation After Lausanne: Radical Evangelical Mission in Global-Local Perspective* (Oxford: Regnum Books, 2008), 4.

[40] Tizon, 4.

[41] Tizon, 4.

[42] J. Thacker, "'The Whole Church': Statement of the Lausanne Theology Working Group," *Evangelical Review of Theology* 34, no. 1 (2010): 4.

[43] Daryl Balia, and Kirsteen Kim, *Witnessing to Christ Today* (Oxford: Regnum, 2010), 213.

[44] Lausanne Movement, *Manila Manifesto*, accessed 21 December 2023, https://lausanne.org/content/manifesto/the-manila-manifesto.

comprehension of the *missio Dei* and presenting the redemption of all of creation through Jesus Christ as the focus of establishing God's kingdom, which seeks to transform all nations. Mission is, therefore, the integration of evangelism and the 'committed engagement' and demonstration of the gospel in the world. Proclamation has social outcomes when people are called to 'love and repentance', and social participation has evangelistic implications when the church bears witness to Christ's 'transforming grace'. Since God has a redemptive plan for all creation, the *Commitment* urges Christians to critical and 'prophetic ecological responsibility' because of the wastage of the earth's resources and corresponding rampant consumerism.[45] There is a coming together of these two strands. Tension continues between these two throughout the evangelical movement regarding how to interpret the *missio Dei*.

Ed Stetzer and Phil Nation emphasise the glorification of the triune God in the *missio Dei* as 'the Father sent the Son to accomplish this redemption, so He sends the Spirit to apply this redemption to the hearts of men and women'.[46] God enables the church in his mission for 'witness and service'.[47] The redemptive movement originates from the triune God, flows through the church into the world, and 'results in people of every tribe, tongue, and nation responding in lifelong worship of God'.[48] The climax of the *missio Dei* occurs when 'God creates a new heaven and new earth'.[49]

Enoch Wan defines mission as 'the Christian (individual) and the church (institutional)' participating in the *missio Dei* of the triune God.[50] This mission has two aspects: 'saving souls [and] ushering in *shalom* [for the] redemption, reconciliation, and transformation' of God's creation.[51]

Michael Gorman states that *missio Dei* is 'what God is up to in the world… in a word, salvation'[52] – the wholistic salvation of all. Despite a wide range of positions within evangelicalism on the nature of mission, the concept of the *missio Dei* – at least in theory – is generally accepted.

---

[45] Lausanne Movement, *Cape Town Commitment*, accessed 21 December 2023, https://lausanne.org/content/ctc/ctcommitment.

[46] Ed Stetzer, and Phil Nation, *The Mission of God: Essays and Letters* (Nashville: LifeWay Press, 2015), 8.

[47] Stetzer, and Nation, 8.

[48] Stetzer, and Nation, 8.

[49] Stetzer, and Nation, 8.

[50] Enoch Wan, "The Trinitarian Nature of the Mission of God," in *The Mission of God: Essays and Letters*, ed. Ed Stetzer and Phil Nation (Nashville: LifeWay Press, 2015), 35.

[51] Wan, in *The Mission of God: Essays and Letters*, 35.

[52] Stroope, 18.

Ecumenical Perspective

The 2012 WCC *Together Towards Life* states that mission is 'not a project of expanding churches',[53] but originates in the heart of the triune God. God is missionary and calls and enables his people to be a community of hope. The gospel as the good news applies to all creation and impacts every part of life and community. Through the power of the Holy Spirit, this community repels and transforms all 'life-destroying forces'.[54]

Reflecting on the centenary of the Edinburgh 1910 World Missionary Conference illuminates the contrast that took place over 100 years of developing a theology of mission. In 1910, the focus was on the '*missions* of the churches [or] church-centred mission'.[55] By 2010, this shifted to God's mission or *missio Dei* – a 'mission-centred church' – in which Christians participate and seek 'missionary collaboration beyond the church'.[56] In 1910, there existed an awareness of the multiplicity of missions. One hundred years later, mission is defined in the singular sense; it is multifaceted and includes 'witness, proclamation, catechesis, worship, inculturation [and] inter-faith dialogue'.[57] Understanding the foundation of God's mission has evolved from 'ecclesiology and soteriology' to a Trinitarian perspective.[58] These are shifts within the ecumenical movement, but at its heart is the *missio Dei*, the God 'who acts in history and in creation' in specific situations for 'the fullness of life for the whole earth through justice, peace, and reconciliation',[59] involving the church as it participates in God's mission, through 'proclamation, … justice and liberation'.[60]

Missio Dei has a two-fold action: (1) a cooperative 'action by Father, Son and Holy Spirit (John 14:26)' and (2) a 'divine action [that] invites human participation… (John 20:21)'. God does not need human instrumentality but 'chooses the risky course of partnership', starting with appointing the first disciples as his co-workers who held different social and theological positions.[61] While evangelicals are, at times, prone to focus exclusively on a personal relationship with the King, sometimes those within the WCC may be in danger of focusing solely on the kingdom, and in so doing, both parties separate the King from the kingdom. A truly holistic recognition of the *missio Dei* will instead bring the two together. Lesslie Newbigin understood that when he said that the kingdom now has a human face – that of Jesus Christ.

---

[53] Jooseop Keum, *Together Towards Life: Mission and Evangelism in Changing Landscapes* (Geneva: WCC Publications, 2013), 60.

[54] Keum, 4.

[55] Balia, and Kim, 11.

[56] Balia, and Kim, 11.

[57] Balia, and Kim, 11.

[58] Balia, and Kim, 23.

[59] Keum, 17.

[60] Balia, and Kim, 15.

[61] Balia, and Kim, 128.

Roman Catholic Viewpoint

At Vatican II (1962–1965), the concept of *missio Dei* gained acceptance, recognising the Roman Catholic Church as missionary by its very nature, drawing its origin from the mission of the Son and the Holy Spirit in agreement with God the Father's command.

Roman Catholic missiologists Stephen Bevans and Roger Schroeder define mission as an interdependent grouping of factors that consist of: 'witness and proclamation; liturgy, prayer, and contemplation; justice, peace, and integrity of creation; interreligious dialogue; inculturation; and reconciliation'.[62]

At Vatican II, much thought was given to the church's relationship to other religions, and a view gained popularity that people could find Christ within their religions. And in 2013, Pope Francis published the apostolic exhortation *Evangelii Gaudium*, 'the joy of the gospel'.[63] Pope Francis called the church back to making 'missionary outreach' its exemplary activity.[64] The church walks in submission to Jesus' command to go and make disciples. The church as 'an evangelizing community gets involved by word and deed in people's daily lives; it bridges distances, it is willing to abase itself if necessary, and it embraces human life, touching the suffering flesh of Christ in others.'[65] 'Evangelization in joy' is liturgical as 'the Church evangelizes and is herself evangelized through the beauty of the liturgy, which is both a celebration of the task of evangelization and the source of her renewed self-giving.'[66] As the church pursues an 'evangelizing fervour', new church institutions, communities and movements arise and benefit from retaining contact with 'the local parish and to participate readily in the overall pastoral activity of the particular Church.'[67]

Eastern Orthodox Approach

In the Eastern Orthodox Church, mission is viewed 'as the very providential intervention of God into history.... Mission is identified with the continuity of the Church over the centuries, with the conveyance of the faith in time, from one generation to another.'[68] Mission was initially driven by sending communities in Europe and North America that influenced contemporary independent Christian movements in Asia, Africa, and South America. The missional focus of the church is 'the life of communion in God... attracting people to the communion with the Holy Trinity.'[69]

---

[62] Bevans, and Schroeder, 4.

[63] Pope Francis, *Apostolic Exhortation Evangelii Gaudium* (The Vatican: Vatican Press, 2013), 3.

[64] Francis, 19.

[65] Francis, 22.

[66] Francis, 23.

[67] Francis, 27.

[68] Cristian Sonea, "*Missio Dei*—the Contemporary Missionary Paradigm and its Reception in the Eastern Orthodox Missionary Theology," *Review of Ecumenical Studies* 9, no. 1 (2017): 77, https://dx.doi.org/10.1515/ress-2017-0006.

[69] Sonea, 90.

Rather than being concerned about geographically expanding the Christian faith through the proclamation of the gospel, the Orthodox churches 'have tried to preserve the true faith in a living continuity along centuries and thus are tempted to focus on those who leave the Church rather than those who are not yet part of it.'[70] People must be drawn to and turn to God through a transforming encounter with the liturgy. This understanding of mission in part stems from being established in the cultures where the church has had a long presence. Mission is 'deeply rooted in the communion of the Holy Trinity, as seen in the love of the Father for the Son within the Holy Spirit, and towards mankind.'[71] Mission only happens within, 'through and for the Church… which is the place where the sanctification of the universe happens.'[72] In other words, mission is not a profession, it is a characteristic of the Church.

Comparing Positions

In 2017, Kenneth Ross did a comparison of Lausanne's *Cape Town Commitment*, the WCC's *Together Towards Life*, and the Vatican's *Evangelii Gaudium*. Essentially, what he found were similarities between the distinct streams of Christianity expressed through these three documents, which represent evangelical, ecumenical, and Roman Catholic positions on the *missio Dei*. Ross found 'thematic convergence' with creation, justice, evangelism, migration, religious plurality, and leadership.[73] He noted commonality in all three documents with these principles:

- 'The primary agent of mission is not human but divine.'[74]
- 'Mission is the concern not of professionals but of disciples.'[75]
- 'Agency in mission is not primarily individual but rather ecclesial.'[76]
- Rather than orthodoxy 'from the head' and orthopraxy 'from the hand', there's 'a new emphasis on the affective or emotional dimension of life… orthopathy… from the heart'.[77]

Summary

In this overview of the theological development of the *missio Dei*, we see how its theological formulation has unfolded since the 1800s. Many factors influenced how theologians and missiologists understood and articulated God's mission. Cultural and contextual issues affected its formulation, while vigorous

---

[70] Sonea, 77.

[71] Sonea, 79.

[72] Sonea, 81.

[73] Kenneth R. Ross, "Understanding Mission Today: Points of Convergence?" *Transformation* 34, no. 4 (2017): 263–65.

[74] Ross, 261.

[75] Ross, 261.

[76] Ross, 262.

[77] Ross, 263.

discussions at regional and global conferences influenced our modern understanding of *missio Dei*. Through the church's ongoing adaptation of theological positions, we gain insights into how these positions change over time and are affected by various events and people. At the same time, we note some discontinuity between the early church and the re-emergence of the term 'mission' that has not necessarily been associated with *missio Dei*. This points to how *missio Dei's* journey of development has certainly not been continuous. Through our study of the term, we can learn to appreciate the depth, richness, and complexity of the term. Now, we can apply this understanding to our mission practice.

Reflective Questions:

- What stands out to you about the *missio Dei* from our overview of its history and theological interpretations?
- What are ways you can apply your understanding of *missio Dei* to your context?

2. Identifying Boundaries in Mission

Introduction

Observing mission past and present informs our understanding of Mission Theology. In this chapter, we examine the concept of paradigms as a way of recognising and interpreting changes in how the church has perceived and participated in God's mission.

David Bosch's 1991 text *Transforming Mission* popularised the use of the word 'paradigm' when referring to the different phases of mission development in church history. Bosch pointed out that paradigms take time, even centuries, to emerge. Since, by its very nature, a paradigm is not static, it traverses through adjustments, or what we call 'paradigm shifts'. Paradigm shifts occur when a considerable alteration happens, with one way of understanding replacing another.

It was evident to Bosch that we live in a time of deep uncertainty and confusion as we navigate mission in and between shifting paradigms. Thirty years after his writing, we still live in that uncertainty and confusion concerning our perception of which paradigm of mission we are currently experiencing. Consequently, we benefit from learning about the historical markers of church and mission history and how they influence the future of mission.

Defining Paradigm

What exactly is a paradigm? American physicist and philosopher Thomas Kuhn's *The Structure of Scientific Revolutions* is considered an authority on the theory of paradigms and paradigm shifts. Kuhn defines a paradigm in two ways: (1) It is a complete collection of 'beliefs, values, techniques, and so on [held by] a given community' and (2) It conveys one 'element' of that collection that can replace any previously held rules as a basis for a new solution or discovery.[1] Theologian Timothy Laniak gives equivalent terms including cultural systems or models, mental models, schemas, frames, prisms, images or symbols, implicit theories, representations, cognitive maps, and assumptions.[2] A paradigm occurs when a community has accepted a particular way of thinking, methodology, framework, or foundational worldview.

When developed, a paradigm provides a valuable tool to comprehend human perspectives and describe sets of experiences, beliefs, and values that affect how

---

[1] Thomas Kuhn, *The Structure of Scientific Revolutions*, 50th anniversary ed. (Chicago: University of Chicago Press, 2012), 174.

[2] Timothy Laniak, *Shepherds After My Own Heart: Pastoral Traditions and Leadership in the Bible* (Downers Grove: InterVarsity Press, 2006), 35.

people perceive and respond to reality. For our purposes, a paradigm in mission is:

- a frame of reference for constructing a way of thinking about a given topic;
- a lens for viewing a new reality;
- a tool that gives a new perspective to an older subject;
- an academic device that enables new definitions in disciplinary activities involving techniques, methods, procedures;
- lenses that help us interpret the boundaries of where we are in mission history and what mission practices are helpful or require change.

Paradigm Shifts

A paradigm shift represents a fundamental transformation in a particular context's basic concepts, practices, beliefs, and methods. The shift begins when a significant change or crisis occurs. The old way of thinking no longer holds up, and a new mode of perceiving reality emerges, replacing the old, making more sense, and providing solutions for the community. By its very nature, a paradigm is not static and is subject to change over time as new theories are tested. There may always be a degree of uncertainty and disorder throughout the shift because remnants of the old may continue to linger, even in the new. Paradigm shifts might occur incrementally – over years or decades – or, in some cases, take place instantaneously. Kuhn focused mainly on the scientific world, but more recently, the idea of paradigms has expanded to include a whole range of human experiences.

When Bosch wrote *Transforming Mission*, he said the church had entered a crisis period because he could see that the old model of understanding, a Christendom model, was giving way to what he described as a new ecumenical model. However, he predicted it would take many decades to be resolved. Bosch stated that 'the magnitude of today's challenge can really only be appreciated if viewed against the backdrop of almost twenty centuries of church history'.[3] The current paradigm may raise questions and challenges for the emerging one and may involve a time of uncertainty and disorder until the community accepts the new paradigm.

The credibility of a new paradigm develops as it is tested and viewed as capable of solving some of the problems that the old one created, and proves helpful with emerging issues. The new paradigm gains trust and popularity as the community engages with it, arrives at new insights, discovers new possibilities, and sees the potential for overcoming barriers. A new paradigm can be viewed as an opportunity for course correction, and in some situations, it may offer a complete change of direction.

---

[3] David Bosch, *Transforming Mission: Paradigm Shifts in Theology of Mission* (Maryknoll: Orbis Books, 2011), 193.

Paradigm Shifts in Christian History

No single theologian, missiologist, or mission agency can create a new paradigm. Instead, it emerges, develops, and matures over time. Intense emotional reactions against the new paradigm arise until it is accepted as credible and supplants the old one. When the community rejects one paradigm and accepts a new one, it is basing this on comparing the new with the old.

Hans Küng notes how a paradigm forms 'in an extraordinary complex of various social, political, ecclesiastical, and theological factors. It grows out of them and matures in them.'[4] In any season of paradigm shift in the history of the church and Christianity, simultaneous effects of continuity and change occur, characterised by faithfulness to tradition and boldness to engage in future transformation. It has participants who continue to operate in the old ways. Today, these could be theologians of the modern era who grew up within the boundaries of the Enlightenment but now find themselves functioning simultaneously in a postmodern paradigm. The result is a kind of 'theological schizophrenia',[5] with the continuation of the Christendom model of mission until there is greater clarity about the new paradigm.

New paradigms take time, even centuries, to emerge, stabilise, and be perceived as the norm. In the process, they can create a time of great uncertainty and confusion. Learning how established paradigms begin to shift is helpful to our interpretation of mission history and practice.

Historical Paradigms of the Church in Mission

To appreciate how paradigm shifts have occurred in the church's history, we look at the eras of mission starting with Jesus, Paul, and the early church up to the early twenty-first century. Options we could use for this historical exploration include following it through chronological eras. Christian historian Dana Robert does this by placing it into three eras: (1) 'From Christ to Christendom'; (2) 'Vernaculars and Volunteers, 1450–'; and (3) 'Global Networking for the Nations, 1910–'.[6] Stephen Neill casts this history in 12 eras from the birth of Christ to '1914 and after'.[7] Others follow a topical approach. For example, Andrew Walls maps this history through cultural themes of transmitting the Christian faith.[8] Ruth Tucker follows the faithfulness of key

---

4 Hans Küng, *Theology for the Third Millennium* (New York: Anchor Books, 1988), 173.
5 Bosch, *Transforming Mission: Paradigm Shifts in Theology of Mission*, 192.
6 Dana Robert, *Christian Mission: How Christianity Became a World Religion* (Chichester: Wiley-Blackwell, 2009), vii.
7 Stephen Neill, *A History of Christian Missions*, 2nd ed. (London: Penguin, 1986).
8 Andrew Walls, *The Missionary Movement in Christian History: Studies in the Transmission of Faith* (Maryknoll: Orbis Books, 1996).

people.[9] John Mark Terry and Robert Gallagher plot it through mission and church structures and movements.[10]

While these methods are valid, we choose to follow theologians Hans Küng and David Bosch's division of the 2,000-year history of Christianity into six major paradigms.[11] Doctrinal, ecclesiological, sociological, political, and cultural elements within each paradigm characterised the epoch and influenced how Christianity was understood and practised. We also draw occasionally from Edward Smither's use of six eras that overlap with Bosch's.[12] Our mapping of these paradigms, or historical formations, follows a Western-centric path from Jerusalem to Northern Europe through Greece and Rome and from there to the rest of the world. This is how Bosch presents it.

(1) Early Christian Apocalyptic Paradigm (30–100 CE)

The early Jewish Christianity paradigm preceded and birthed the New Testament. It occurred during the dominant context of the Roman Empire and Hellenistic culture, first-century Christianity, and the beginning of Jewish Christendom in Jerusalem, Palestine, and Mesopotamia. In that early phase recorded in the Scriptures, primarily led by Jesus and the apostles, and later, Paul and his missionary bands, the church began as a Jewish sect. It quickly broadened to a path where all ethnic groups could find their way in Christ, an extraordinary breakthrough in understanding and becoming God's people.

Paul presents a great example of a cross-cultural mission or missionary. His approach is significant. He was at least bi-cultural, if not tri-cultural: a Jew and a Roman citizen who grew up among the Greeks, speaking Hebrew, Greek, and probably Latin. He aimed for urban centres, synagogues, and those who feared God and acted as bridge-builders between minority Jew and majority Gentile culture. We suggest the intention of this approach was more theological than strategic: the Jews – his own people – first, then the Gentiles. Some other examples:

- In Acts 13:49, we read that the word of the Lord spread through the region, partly through Paul's work, but mainly through individual Christians and family groups connecting across their social networks. A small, fragile worshipping community established in urban centres supported Paul's assertion that the whole region had heard the gospel. Donald McGavran portrayed the gospel as communicating through existing networks and lines

---

[9] Ruth Tucker, *From Jerusalem to Irian Jaya: A Biographical History of Christian Missions*, 2nd ed. (Grand Rapids: Zondervan, 2004).

[10] John Mark Terry, and Robert Gallagher, *Encountering the History of Missions: From the Early Church to Today* (Grand Rapids: Baker Academic, 2017).

[11] Küng, 128. Bosch, *Transforming Mission: Paradigm Shifts in Theology of Mission*, 185.

[12] Edward Smither, *Christian Mission: A Concise Global History* (Bellingham: Lexham Press, 2019).

of communication.[13] Similarly, sociologist Rodney Stark described the first couple of centuries when the church was located throughout the Roman Empire, revealing the convergence between where the church and a large Jewish diaspora existed.[14]

• Romans 1:8 and 1 Thessalonians 1:8 describe how the believers' faith was being reported all over the known world. Even in New Testament times, the gospel spread mainly through means other than the Acts 13 model of being sent. When Paul presents the approach of going first to the Jew and then the Gentile, he's not driven by a modernistic understanding of strategy development but by a theological paradigm: that the gospel has come first to the Jews and then to the Gentiles. In the first century and beyond comes the expansion through social networks.

• In Acts 8:1b, 8:4, and 11:19-20, the diaspora Jews and those who feared God were scattered throughout the region and 'preached the word wherever they went' (8:4). When they were all gathered together and heard that early Pentecost proclamation, about three thousand souls were added (Acts 2). Many would return to their homes throughout the Roman Empire, taking the gospel with them.

• The powerful work of the Holy Spirit moved the people of God, including through persecution. In Acts 8:1b, all except the apostles were scattered. Paul and his companions in Acts 16 were all 'rerouted'. Willie James Jennings notes how the story of Acts is the story of the Holy Spirit 'always… pressing the disciples to go to those to whom they would in fact strongly prefer never to share space, or a meal, and definitely not life together'.[15] No organised human strategy for cross-cultural mission was apparent.

• Christians of this era thought Christ's return and the end of the age would come soon in their lifetime. This was evident in John's vision in Revelation: 'This is a revelation from Jesus Christ, which God gave him to show his servants the events that must soon take place' (Acts 1:1).

We often focus on the work of the Apostle Paul through his ministry and teaching, recorded in the book of Acts. There we gain insight into the nature of the gospel, Paul's epistles, and the critical issue of how and when the church changes from being the people of God – a Jewish people of God – into one for all ethnicities.

(2) Early Church Hellenistic Paradigm (First to Seventh Centuries)

This epoch coincides with Greek Orthodoxy and the Byzantine Empire. Christianity rapidly became 'Hellenised' and 'desemitised' as its centre moved

---

[13] Donald A. McGavran, *Bridges of God: A Study in the Strategy of Missions* (Eugene: Wipf & Stock Publishers, 2005).

[14] Rodney Stark, *The Rise of Christianity: A Sociologist Reconsiders History* (Princeton: Princeton University Press, 1996).

[15] Willie James Jennings, *Acts—Belief: A Theological Commentary on the Bible* (Louisville: Westminister John Knox Press, 2017), 11.

from Jerusalem to Rome and Christianity expanded from the land of its birth. Matthew Burden notes how 'the Mediterranean world had never seen something like this', since the region was marked by its pluralistic gods.[16] Instead, people of the region were confronted with 'a faith which claimed the prerogative of total and exclusive allegiance – not only over its own people but over all people'.[17]

This second paradigm brought ecclesial hierarchy to the church with the rule of bishops and, ultimately, the emperor. Further, it subjugated Christian theology to Greek philosophy, most notably in its conciliar definitions of the Trinity and Christology brought about by the early church councils. The challenge for the early church was not just survival but growth.

During the first and second centuries, there was *paradosis* (tradition of instruction) of the *patres* (church fathers), early Catholicism, and the rise of Gnosticism (personal spiritual knowledge – gnosis – over orthodox teachings) and persecutions.

Leaders encompassed Greek and Latin church fathers, including Origen (185–254 CE), who was born in Alexandria, Egypt, and Cyprian (200–258 CE, bishop of Carthage). Cyprian is famous for his foundation of Christian ethics: 'We do not speak great things, we live them.' He also wrote *Ad Quirinium Book Three* (240 CE), a catechetical document containing 120 precepts with two functions: they helped form a distinctive community that aided catechumens in memorising Scripture and they covered categories of belief, belonging, and behaviour. There were topics of non-violence, care for the sick, integrity, refusal to take vows, equality, and the kiss of peace (i.e. Precept 1: The benefits of good works and mercy). Each was backed up with biblical texts.[18]

Tertullian (155–220 CE) was a significant figure in early Christian theology. He, like Cyprian, was from North Africa, which 'had given birth to some of the finest Latin Christian theology'.[19] Tertullian, a leader of the church of North Africa, wrote in Latin, making him one of the earliest Christian writers to do so. His works were instrumental in spreading Christian thinking in the Western Roman Empire and the growing influence of the Latin language on theology.

Anthony the Great (251–356 CE) was an Egyptian monk and one of the Desert Fathers. They practised a form of monasticism with a rigorous ascetic lifestyle which emerged in the deserts and regions of North Africa. Some monks ventured into nearby regions and beyond 'and enhanced African missionary successes in Nubia, Sudan, and Ethiopia'.[20]

Other leaders included Athanasius (296–373 CE) and the Cappadocians, Basil of Caesarea (330–379 CE), Gregory of Nyssa (335–395 CE), and Gregory of Nazianzus (329–389 CE). The Cappadocia region (in what is now Türkiye) was

---

[16] Matthew Burden, *Missionary Motivations: Challenges from the Early Church* (Littleton: William Carey Publishing, 2023), 1.

[17] Burden, 1.

[18] Alan Kreider, *The Patient Ferment of the Early Church: The Improbable Rise of Christianity in the Roman Empire* (Grand Rapids: Baker Academic, 2016), 161–70.

[19] Miram Adeney, "Algeria," in *Evangelical Dictionary of World Missions*, ed. A. Scott Moreau (Grand Rapids: Baker, 2000), 53.

[20] J. Ray Tallman, "Egypt," in *Evangelical Dictionary of World Missions*, 305.

an early site of Christian activity at the time of the Apostle Paul's missions. The Cappadocians advanced the development of early Christian theology, including the topic of the Trinity, and were respected church fathers in both Western and Eastern churches.

Augustine (354–430 CE) was another of the early leaders. He was born in Roman North Africa (modern-day Algeria) and received his early education in Africa, including studying rhetoric in Carthage. Tertullian, Augustine, Cyprian, and Origen all lived in North Africa during different periods of the early Christian era.

Another leader of the era was Gregory I (540–604 CE). He led the first large-scale mission from Rome, often referred to as the Gregorian Mission, to convert pagan Anglo-Saxons in England to Christianity.

As Christianity spread, momentum developed and political interest in the phenomenon heightened. By the mid-fourth century, the Roman emperor Constantine declared Christianity the state religion. Rodney Stark estimates that by that time, probably 10% of the Roman Empire had become Christian – an extraordinary growth in the size of the church.[21] Constantine the Great (306–337 CE) played an influential role in the proclamation of the Edict of Milan in 313, which declared tolerance for Christianity in the Roman Empire. He convoked the First Council of Nicaea in 325, which produced the statement of Christian belief known as the Nicene Creed as a response to settling the divine nature of God the Son and his relationship to God the Father. On Constantine's orders, the Church of the Holy Sepulchre was built at the purported site of Jesus' tomb in Jerusalem and became the holiest place in the Christian world. Constantine has historically been referred to as the 'First Christian Emperor', and he did favour the Christian church, granting it imperial power and alignment, giving rise to the term 'Christendom' as referring to this special status of the church and its participants. He converted to Christianity on his deathbed.

Roman historian Ramsay MacMullen, reviewing the church's extraordinary growth, observed that up until the conversion of Constantine, power was primarily located in the miraculous.[22] The early Christians demonstrated God's presence through miracles, which attracted people. As a secular historian, MacMullen warns us not to view that through our twentieth-century – now twenty-first century – eyes but to accept the worldview of that time. He then remarks on the power of miracles being transformed into the power of the state and the state imposing Christianity as it did in the fifth to the ninth centuries.

When Michael Green explored this concept, he considered evangelism and apologetics the critical factors. The early church actively shared its faith, producing apologetic materials addressing why it was right to follow Christ and countering the accusations against the church. However, in his book *The Patient Ferment of the Early Church*, Alan Kreider points out that church documents of the first four centuries demonstrate no thesis and no clear argument specifying

---

[21] Stark, 7.

[22] MacMullen, *Corruption and the Decline of Rome* (New York: Yale University Press, 1988).

evangelism and apologetics as the strategy to grow the church – far from it.[23] Instead, he relates, somewhat ironically, that the first thesis on evangelism and apologetics recognised in the early church is Michael Green's in the twentieth century. How does Kreider, using his research, explain this dramatic explosion of the early church? It all comes down to the quality of discipleship. Christians were different. They lived differently as a counter-cultural community, which was so powerful and attractive that despite no clear strategy for growth, it was through faithful discipleship that the church grew.

The story of the Eastern church differs from that of the Western church. As Christianity expanded eastwards into Persia, Armenia, and Georgia in the third and fourth centuries, various factors emerged, including missionary monks and migrants. There are some examples of people sent by the church, but it was mainly migrants, including stories of slaves who carried the gospel to the new lands to which they were taken. Additionally, the translation of the Bible into vernacular languages was of great significance. A Coptic translation was produced for Egyptians in the middle of the third century CE. Other regional translations were done for the Sahidic and Bohairic languages, also in Egypt. Mesrop Mashtots assembled various manuscripts translated by scholars in the Armenian language and is credited with translating the Bible into Armenian in the early fifth century. Methodius and Cyril worked on a translation for the Slavonic languages in the late ninth century.

Michael Green notes how the early church was known for emphasising evangelism to the extent that 'this tiny band of men and women in a fringe province of the far-flung Roman Empire became a world faith within a few generations'.[24] Alan Kreider observes that the early believers took seriously Jesus' 'summons to discipleship'.[25] This included the Apostle Paul, who 'dramatized the costs – conversion entailed the death of sinful patterns of living – and the rewards – there was rebirth to life under a new Lord as "slaves of righteousness" (Rom. 6:18). Conversion meant change.'[26] Lives that were different: behaving according to living like Christ meant people were 'intrigued… at the God whom the Christians [said] motivates their behavior'.[27]

It is uncertain how Christianity arrived in India, but quite possibly through Christian believers fleeing persecution from the Sassanid Persian rulers in third-century Persia, taking the gospel with them. Earlier in the first century, the Apostle Thomas went to Malabar on the west coast of India where, through his preaching, churches were established. When the Portuguese arrived in India in the early 1600s, they found a group of Christians called the Malankara Mar Thoma Syrian Church, which traced its roots to Thomas in 56 CE.

---

[23] Kreider.

[24] Michael Green, *Evangelism in the Early Church* (Grand Rapids: Wm B. Eerdmans, 2004), 14.

[25] Alan Kreider, *The Change of Conversion and the Origin of Christendom* (Eugene: Wipf & Stock, 1999), 11.

[26] Kreider, *The Change of Conversion and the Origin of Christendom*, 11.

[27] Kreider, *The Patient Ferment of the Early Church: The Improbable Rise of Christianity in the Roman Empire*, 15.

Christianity arrived in post-biblical Ethiopia through the shipwreck of two brothers, Frumentius and Edesius. They were shipwrecked and imprisoned on the East African coast but shared their faith and soon won favour with the local king. They then organised Christian traders and began a Christian community. Frumentius served as its first bishop in Aksum (Axum) around 325 CE, still considered the centre of Ethiopian orthodoxy.

During the Celtic era, 300–500 CE, monasteries and monks formed Christian communities with a similar focus on community as the early church. Monasticism was very important in advance of the gospel during this period. Monks sent out other monks, who left home for new lands to set up new Christian monastic communities. Writers have pointed out that the Celtic movement was as much an act of renunciation as it was mission or evangelisation.[28] Stroope observes that you cannot read back our modern-day understanding of mission into what the Celts were doing.[29] They were creating communities that became places of study, discipline, prayer, discipleship, healing, and service to the local community and preparing the next group to be sent out. These communities became attractive places where people encountered the Christian faith and began following Christ. There were similarities to mission of the Orthodox church. For example, John of Chrysostom, one of the founders of the Eastern Orthodox communities of churches, explains that mission and monastery must go together. The lesson in terms of reaching out is in the means of community that is both monastic and missionary – a powerful dyad.

Edward Smither refers to this era as 'Mission in the Early Church', characterised by the sending of 'unnamed, itinerant evangelists to travel and cross cultures to proclaim the gospel'.[30] Alan Kreider describes this growth of the early church as God's 'patient ferment' that was 'brewing, but not under anyone's control. It was uncoordinated, it was unpredictable, and it seemed unstoppable' and the faith of the early Christians 'was attractive to people who were dissatisfied with their old cultural and religious habits' and were pulled toward a new life in Christ'.[31] Carlos Cardoza-Orlandi and Justo Gonzáles also note the missionary methods of this paradigm show no particular formal strategy for mission:

> These methods reflect a genuine interest in sharing the faith in various circumstances and places, frequently making use of the cultural and social structures of each group or society as channels for communication. One of the most remarkable characteristics of this period is the almost total absence of 'missionaries' – that is, people sent by the church to teach the faith elsewhere.... Perhaps all of the above indicates that a truly missionary church does not seek to discharge its responsibilities by placing it on the shoulders of missionaries or by

---

[28] Bosch, *Transforming Mission: Paradigm Shifts in Theology of Mission*, 230–36.
[29] Stroope, 111–18.
[30] Smither, 39.
[31] Kreider, *The Patient Ferment of the Early Church: The Improbable Rise of Christianity in the Roman Empire*, 12.

limiting it to a particular moment of its life but by itself becoming an instrument of its missionary vocation.[32]

Preaching and worship were not the main methods of conversion. During this era, there was no formal strategy for mission as we would identify it today. With one or two exceptions, the established church had little to do with missionary spread.

(3) Medieval Roman Catholic Paradigm
(Eighth to Fifteenth Centuries)

This epoch, also known as the Middle Ages, was characterised by the Latinisation of Christianity. According to Edward Smither, this was the era of 'Mission in the Medieval Church'.[33] The translation of the Christian vernacular Scriptures from Greek to Latin influenced the church. This era saw the gospel expanding 'to the rest of Western Europe, while reaching new regions such as Scandinavia, Eastern Europe and Russia, the Middle East, North Africa, and Central Asia'.[34]

A result of the Gregorian reforms (1050–80 CE) attributed to Pope Gregory VII was the centralisation of church leadership through the papacy and the office of the Pope. Consequently, the bishop of Rome assumed primacy over all the other bishops and the emperor. This led to Pope Innocent III (1198–1216 CE) becoming one of the most powerful and influential medieval popes, exerting authority over the Christian states of Europe and claiming supremacy over all of Europe's kings. The Latin church emerged as the dominant form of Christianity throughout the Middle Ages. Augustine of Hippo is this epoch's defining figure, with Thomas Aquinas also having a considerable impact. These and other church leaders attempted 'to create a Christian civilization, to shape laws consonant with biblical teaching [and] to place kings and emperors under the explicit obligation of Christian discipleship'.[35] North Africa held one of the largest Christian communities in the western part of the Roman Empire. However, within two centuries, Christianity there 'buckled and almost completely disappeared in the face of... Muslim invasions'.[36]

The Crusades are a primary part of history associated with this era. Pope Urban II called for the first Crusade at the Council of Clermont in 1095 to provide the Byzantine emperor Alexios with military support against the Seljuk Turks' occupation of Jerusalem. On 15 July 1099, 'a great host of warriors drawn from across the Latin West' followed the familiar path of pilgrims, arrived in Jerusalem, and 'stormed its walls. The city was theirs.' Tom Holland notes how

---

[32] Carlos F. Cardoza-Orlandi, and Justo L. Gonzáles, *To All Nations, From All Nations: A History of the Christian Missionary Movement* (Nashville: Abingdon Press, 2013), 67–68.
[33] Smither, v.
[34] Smither, 49.
[35] Bosch, *Transforming Mission: Paradigm Shifts in Theology of Mission*, 237.
[36] Burden, 55.

they gathered at the 'tomb of Christ [and] there, in joy and disbelief, they offered up praises to God. Jerusalem – after centuries of Saracen rule – was Christian once again.'[37] Subsequent crusades as religious wars in Europe and the Holy Lands continued until 1699, with a range of religious motivations, such as participants being offered penitence that brought absolution of their sins to political motivations that included expanding the territory of Christendom.

The Great East–West Schism of 1054 was the break of communion between what is now the Roman Catholic Church and the Eastern Orthodox churches due to the culmination of theological and political differences that had developed over the preceding centuries. This significant development would shape people, nations, and politics for centuries to come – even to the present.

The medieval Catholic Church's zeal and desire for power and control led to historical notoriety with the Holy Inquisition of the twelfth century. It began in France and was led by the institutions of the Catholic Church, aiming to combat heresy within the church. Torture and violence were used to elicit confessions from those accused of being heretics.

The Renaissance took place in Europe from the fourteenth to seventeenth centuries. It marked the interest in art and literature through cultural, artistic, and economic rebirth following the fall of Rome in 476 CE as the start of the Middle Ages, which continued to the sixteenth century. 'Old ways and beliefs were abandoned, forsaken for something better, something promising, something hopeful.... Real-life representations in paintings replaced medieval iconic figures.... Every part of culture was changed, including the church.'[38]

Scholasticism emerged as a form of medieval philosophy closely affiliated with the Christian monastic schools and became the basis of the earlier European universities. This was initially led by Bonaventure (1221–1274), who was considered to be the greatest philosopher of the Middle Ages and whose writings integrated philosophy with theology.

This era under review is also known as the Dark Ages, especially up to 1,000 CE. It was called so because of the collapse of the Roman Empire and 'more frequent encounters with Goths, Muslims, and later, Vikings, [who were] regarded as barbaric, uncivilized hordes.'[39] Mission in this season was characterised by disorder as some rulers coerced their subjects into Christianity, while there were also missionaries who remained true to biblical and missional motivations. These dedicated servants of God were crucial in safeguarding a portion of the church during the medieval era.

In Jehu Hanciles' exploration of the pre-1500 period, he concludes that Christianity grew primarily 'through the agency and activity of migrants – individuals and communities living as strangers and outsiders in foreign lands'.[40]

---

[37] Tom Holland, *Dominion: The Making of the Western Mind* (London: Little, Brown, 2019), 217.

[38] Reggie McNeal, *Missional Renaissance: Changing the Scorecard for the Church* (San Francisco: Jossey-Bass, 2009), 3.

[39] Smither, 49.

[40] Jehu Hanciles, *Migration and the Making of Global Christianity* (Grand Rapids: Wm B. Eerdmans, 2021), 420.

(4) Reformation Protestant Paradigm (Sixteenth Century)

The ideological concept of 'Padroado', well underway by this time, underpinned the fifteenth- to eighteenth-century practice of European colonial expansion, starting with Portugal and its 'intimate relationship between cross and crown [that] shaped efforts at spreading Christianity'.[41]

In the sixteenth century, a split over the Word of God and inerrancy occurred in the Western church, causing the tipping point that led to the Reformation. Reformation orthodoxy's five pillars were *sola Scriptura* (Scripture alone), *sola gratia* (grace alone), *sola fide* (faith alone), *solus Christus* (Christ alone), and *soli Deo gloria* (glory to God alone), with *sola fide* representing the doctrine of justification by faith alone. Pietism arose, focusing on biblical doctrine with Reformed theology and practice emphasising individual piety and living a virtuous Christian life.

In response to the Protestant Reformation, the Roman Catholic Church's Council of Trent met in three parts spread between 1545–1563. Instigated by Pope Paul III, this became known as the Counter-Reformation. The Council defined the heresies committed by proponents of Protestantism, making statements of the church's doctrine and teachings, including Scripture, the biblical canon (with the Vulgate as the official text), sacred tradition, original sin, justification, salvation, the sacraments, the Mass, and the veneration of saints.

Leaders of this era included Protestants Martin Luther, Ulrich Zwingli, John Calvin, Thomas Cranmer, and Thomas Cromwell. Cranmer helped build the case for the annulment of Henry VIII's marriage to Catherine, one of the causes of the separation of the English Church from union with the Holy See. Cromwell supported Royal Supremacy, where the king was considered sovereign over the church within his realm.

The reformers stood up to the church clergy who 'had elevated tradition and its magisterium [*institutional authority*] to the level of Scripture'.[42] Martin Luther and the reformers' determination was marked by their zeal to 'do the right things for the right reasons – all for the glory of God'.[43]

The emergence of Protestantism 'did not translate into a viable global mission movement'.[44] That began in the 1700s through the Moravians. Originally from the Kingdom of Bohemia (Czech Kingdom), they experienced war, persecution, and suffering, and sought refuge on the estates of Count Zinzendorf at Herrnhut. He became their spiritual leader. Count Zinzendorf was influenced by Pietism and had a deep experience of Christ. In 1732, the Moravians began going out as

---

[41] Jehu Hanciles, *Beyond Christendom: Globalization, African Migration, and the Transformation of the West* (Maryknoll: Orbis Books, 2008), 92.

[42] David Barrett, *God's Word Alone: The Authority of Scripture* (Grand Rapids: Zondervan, 2016), 21.

[43] David Steele, *Bold Reformer: Celebrating the Gospel-Centred Convictions of Martin Luther*, Kindle ed. (Houston: Lucid Books, 2016), 158.

[44] Smither, 75.

self-supporting missionaries. Edward Smither notes how 'a high percentage of Moravian believers – about one in 60 – served as cross-cultural missionaries'.[45]

(5) Enlightenment Modern Paradigm
(Seventeenth to Nineteenth Centuries)

The seventeenth to eighteenth centuries, sometimes called the Age of Reason, gave rise to the Enlightenment era in the eighteenth century, recognised for its idealism and humanism. The Enlightenment centred on the importance of reason and evidence of the senses as primary sources of knowledge. The vision was to advance ideals of liberty, progress, tolerance, constitutional government, and separation of church and state.

Ideas about limits to human endeavours were removed and optimism reigned. And the 'whole earth could be occupied and subdued with boldness'.[46] As Stephen Neill observed, 'Christianity was carried forward on the wave of Western prestige and power.'[47] This led to a 'manifest destiny' point of view – thinking that God entrusted the responsibility of making the world a better place to a chosen people. As a result, Bosch stated, 'It was only to be expected that the nationalistic spirit would, in due time, be absorbed into missionary ideology, and Christians of a specific nation would develop the conviction that they had an exceptional role to play in the advancement of the kingdom of God through the missionary enterprise.'[48]

The rise of manifest destiny conveyed the 'belief that God had chosen specific (Anglo-Saxon) nations, because of their unique or superior qualities, to fulfill his purpose in the world [and] resulted in a potent mix of racial superiority, territorial aggression or colonial expansion'.[49] Similarly, there was also 'divine providence', a theory held by nineteenth-century British evangelicals who believed that their nation's overseas 'territorial possessions reflected God's providence and purpose'.[50] The related idea of the 'white man's burden' proposed that modern Western culture should become the world's culture because the former was 'destined to exercise dominance over others for the latter's own good'.[51] For many years, these theories were significant influences, sometimes outrightly and sometimes subconsciously, in church and mission. But these ideologies would likewise be shaken as the church grew faster outside of Western Christendom and 'entered into African religious cultures and Chinese Confucian cultures, and in each context the local cultures [were] being remade'.[52]

---

[45] Smither, 96.
[46] Bosch, *Transforming Mission: Paradigm Shifts in Theology of Mission*, 264.
[47] Neill, 414.
[48] Bosch, *Transforming Mission: Paradigm Shifts in Theology of Mission*, 299.
[49] Hanciles, 165.
[50] Hanciles, 164.
[51] Hanciles, 170.
[52] Scott Sunquist, *The Unexpected Christian Century* (Grand Rapids: Baker Academic, 2015), 151.

The climate was right for new ideas to flourish in this era. Radical, creative, independent thinking began to undermine the authority of the monarchy and the church, paving the way for political revolutions, including two of the most historically noteworthy. The American Revolution arose from the colonial revolt against Great Britain and established a new nation with a federal government. With its overthrow of the monarchy, the French Revolution led to the first French Republic, ongoing turmoil, and the resulting Napoleonic dictatorship.

Towards the end of the Renaissance, another type of revolution was underway, with events that marked the emergence of modern science led by Nicolaus Copernicus, Galileo Galilei, Christiaan Huygens, and Isaac Newton. The new developments in mathematics, physics, astronomy, biology, human anatomy, and chemistry transformed society's views concerning nature.

Also increasing were industrialisation (leading to the Industrial Revolution), democratisation, nationalism, liberalism, and socialism. Large-scale manufacturing and technical expertise contributed substantially to the Industrial Revolution, yielding commercially viable outcomes. Democratisation sought to bring political and social equality for all. Nationalism focused on the aspirations of one's own country. Liberalism was the political and moral philosophy based on liberty, consent of the governed, and equality before the law with free market and trade, limited government, individual rights, capitalism, democracy, and freedom of speech. In contrast, socialism was about the social ownership of economic and social systems.

Edward Smither notes how 'shifts in thought, including Darwinism [influenced by Charles Darwin and his theory of the origins of species] and biblical higher criticism caused many Christians to embrace liberal theology. They rejected the historic teachings of Scripture… and the exclusive claims of Christianity (Christ is the only way to God).'[53] The development of higher criticism was led by German theologian, philosopher, and biblical scholar Friedrich Schleiermacher and his work integrating the Enlightenment and Protestant Christianity. As a result, he became known as the father of hermeneutics and liberal theology. The influence on a theology of mission was to 'redefine Christian mission as focusing entirely on human social needs. [By] emphasizing humankind's goodness, some missionaries no longer challenged non-believers to repent and believe the gospel but instead pursue a full humanity.'[54]

In this era of European colonial expansion, civilisation, and Christianisation, most scholars considered it a time when mission began to develop into what we understand today. It was built on foundations that included the following:

- Papal bulls (a moral and legal framework) from Pope Nicholas V in 1452 and 1455 granted Portugal and Spain the right to conquer and evangelise new lands and the authority to enslave non-Christians.
- Pope Alexander VI, through a bull in 1493, divided the newly discovered lands outside Europe between Spain and Portugal. He sanctioned military

---

[53] Smither, 149.
[54] Smither, 149.

expansion and colonisation in 'the New World', as long as the people subdued were introduced to the faith.

• The founding of the Jesuits in 1540 by Ignatius of Loyola resulted in evangelism in the Roman Catholic Counter-Reformation era. By 1626 they had 15,000 members (all male) and 440 colleges.

• Enculturation, a feature of mission beginning in the early centuries, encouraged missionaries to learn the language, culture, values, and worldviews of the cultures they were trying to reach.

Protestants only became involved in mission in the eighteenth century, about 200 years after the Reformation. The vehicle for mission became the voluntary society (built on the trading company concept), beginning in earnest in the 1780s, including the birth of the London Missionary Society (LMS) in 1795 and the Church Missionary Society (CMS) in 1799.

The birth of the modern mission movement ('an invented tradition, a rhetorical construction'[55]) is generally credited to William Carey (1761–1834) of England and the formation of the Baptist Society for Propagating the Gospel Among the Heathens. Carey wrote *Enquiry into the Obligation of Christians to Use Means for the Propagation of the Gospel Amongst the Heathens* (1792), considered the 'charter for the modern missionary movement'.[56] Carey's thesis, based on Matthew 28:18-20, was to determine whether the Lord's commission to the disciples was still binding, to consider the practicability of doing more in mission, and to discuss the duty of Christians on this matter. The booklet acted as a catalyst, motivating Christians in the US and UK to fulfil the 'Great Commission'. Andrew Walls explains how Carey's views saw the formation of mission societies for the specific purpose and 'efficient means of achieving certain ends: sending and equipping people for the purpose of Christian proclamation and service overseas, and mustering "home" interest and support for their work'.[57]

The Student Volunteer Movement for Foreign Missions was founded in the US in 1886 and combined with rapidly growing Bible institutes and nondenominational or interdenominational faith mission agencies. They emphasised the historic tenets of the Christian faith, including proclaiming the gospel, with a focus on Matthew 28:18-20 as the text of the Great Commission (with influence from Matt. 24:14 and Mark 16:15).

Other Western mission 'greats' included:

• Adoniram Judson (1788–1850), Burma;

• Robert Morrison (1782–1834), China;

• Robert Moffat (1795–1883), South Africa;

• David Livingstone (1813–1873), who went to Africa as a 'missionary explorer' and medical missionary;

• John Geddie (1815–1872), New Hebrides (Vanuatu);

---

[55] Stroope, 321–22.

[56] Leon McBeth, *The Baptist Heritage* (Nashville: Broadman, 1987), 185.

[57] Walls, *The Missionary Movement in Christian History: Studies in the Transmission of Faith*, 260.

- Henry Martyn (1781–1812), Middle East;
- Hudson Taylor (1832–1905), China;
- Charlotte Diggs (Lottie) Moon (1840–1912), China.

Mission theorists Henry Venn (1796–1873) of the CMS in Great Britain and Rufus Anderson (1796–1880) of the American Board of Commissioners for Foreign Missions in the United States 'sought to clarify the main goal of mission and the most effective means of reaching it'.[58] Eventually, the two 'harmonized their thinking' by corresponding with each other about 'the necessity of planting "three self" churches – churches that should be self-supporting, self-governing, and self-propagating'.[59] John L. Nevius (1829–1893), who developed principles based on his work in China called the Nevius Plan, built upon Anderson's and Venn's work. Roland Allen (1868–1947) was an Anglican missionary in China with the Society for the Propagation of the Gospel in Foreign Parts and wrote *Missionary Methods: St Paul's or Ours* in 1912. He, like Nevius, offered five principles for church planting. But what stands out is how he 'consistently emphasized the role of the Holy Spirit in missions and encouraged missionaries to work primarily in itinerant church planting, trusting the Holy Spirit to develop the churches'.[60]

The Protestant missionary movement was led by ordinary people who made extraordinary sacrifices in leaving their home countries for the cause of mission. While doing so, they often found themselves in an uneasy and complex relationship with European colonial expansion. These missionaries led many initiatives, including education, health, agriculture, and poverty alleviation. They brought compassion and service alongside civilisation.

J. Herbert Kane and Andrew Porter 'claim that other lesser-known, non-English-speaking individuals… should be placed at the head of the modern missionary movement [such as] Bartholomäus Ziegenbalg (1683–1719) and Heinrich Plütschau (1677–1752) [both German missionaries to South India] [or] the [German] Moravians [1730s]'.[61] Majority World mission 'greats' included Samuel (Ajayi) Crowther (1807–1891), who originated and served in Nigeria. There were other missionaries from around the world, many of whom substantially impacted their home country and the country where they served. Perhaps less interconnected than the English-speaking participants, they are often not noted as part of a significant movement.

(6) Contemporary Ecumenical Paradigm
(Twentieth to Early Twenty-First Centuries)

Historian Andrew Walls observes two simultaneous approaches to mission contributing to the expansion of the Christian faith that influenced this era – the

---

[58] Wilbert Shenk, "Henry Venn," in *Biographical Dictionary of Christian Missions*, ed. G. Anderson (Grand Rapids: Wm B. Eerdmans, 1998), 698.
[59] Terry, and Gallagher, 259.
[60] Terry, and Gallagher, 261.
[61] Stroope, 321–22.

'crusading mode and the missionary mode'.[62] The former referred to missionary efforts aligned with colonial Christendom governments, comparing God's mission to military conquest and a resulting expansion of territory. Christianity was thought to be a superior faith and would Christianise entire people groups. The latter occurred when missionaries sought to proclaim the gospel and seek out new followers to disciple in their faith sincerely and truthfully. The line between the two approaches is often blurred. The following overview of this paradigm will show how some of this unfolded.

(1) Western leadership of mission to internationalisation of mission

The century began with the famous Edinburgh World Missionary Conference of 1910. Its tone represented Western mission as a formidable force and the expectation that other world religions would die in the face of the triumphant worldwide spread of Christianity. Noticeable optimistic thinking flowed through the discussions and plans for worldwide evangelisation. The Great Commission was positioned as 'an inner principle of church faith and life allowing for freedom in the way churches and missions interpret and carry it out'.[63] 'Christianity appeared to be ascending and moving from triumph to triumph.'[64] Those present at the conference would be responsible for initiating a comprehensive plan for evangelisation that would see the entire world 'reached' in the foreseeable future.[65] The language of world dominion echoed through the corridors, with references, strategies, and plans that used military metaphors, such as crusade, conquest, and advance, based on the prevailing mood that fulfilling God's mission would be a sign of world conquest.

The tone of optimism from Edinburgh in 1910 didn't last, however, when faced with these calamities:

- World War I (1914–1918), with the clash between the Allies and the Central Powers, swept Europe, involving the US and other parts of the Western world.
- Following the Russian Revolution in 1917, Marxist Communism rapidly increased.
- Spanish Flu (H1N1 virus, 1918) infected 500 million people, killing somewhere between 17 and 50 million.
- The Great Depression (1929–1933), triggered by the stock market crash of 29 October 1929, quickly spread to other Western countries over the next decade.
- World War II (1939–1945) involved the great powers aligned in two opposing military groupings, the Allies and the Axis. At its peak, more than 100 million people served in military units. The maps of the world were re-

---

[62] Walls, "Afterword: Christian Mission in a Five-Hundred-Year Context," in *Mission in the 21st Century*, 196.

[63] David Hesselgrave, "The Great Commission," in *Evangelical Dictionary of World Missions*, ed. Scott Moreau (Grand Rapids: Baker Books, 2000), 413.

[64] Terry, and Gallagher, 273.

[65] Noll, 264.

drawn, at least temporarily, as countries such as France, Germany, Japan, and Russia conquered new territories. The US emerged from World War II as the leading world power, although the USSR soon proved to be a strong rival and a threat to world peace.

The British Empire peaked in 1922, at which point it claimed about one-fifth of the world's population. The phrase 'the sun never sets on the British Empire' appropriately described its global reach during that era. But as British world power declined, other nations took a more vital role with missions alongside Britain.

In the US and other Western nations, fundamentalists, and later evangelicals, saw themselves as responsible for bringing the Great Commission to completion by making 'Jesus King' throughout non-Christian lands.[66] Many were key leaders of the rise of the faith mission movement – nondenominational mission agencies forming in response to the Great Commission. Some were specialised, like MAF, Wycliffe Bible Translators, and various radio ministries. The era was 'marked by a great deal of innovation and new strategies',[67] with missionaries personifying 'a near legendary role'.[68] Churches were planted and educational institutions established themselves, 'closely patterned on Western models, funded by Western money, and controlled by Western personnel'.[69]

A rising vision for ecumenism, indicating a call for 'co-operation and unity' in mission, included founding the WCC in 1948.[70] The WCC now comprised the Assyrian Church of the East, Oriental Orthodox Church, much of the Eastern Orthodox Church, Mar Thoma Syrian Church of Malabar, Old Catholic Church, Pentecostals, and the mainline Protestant churches such as Anglican Communion, Lutheran, Mennonite, Methodist, Moravian, Reformed, and Baptist.

Those who served in World War II or the Korean War provided a multitude of recruits for mission agencies in the 1950s and 1960s. They, and much of the rest of the world, were accustomed to military terminology, which quickly found its way into missions and business contexts. Such use of military terms, including base, target, furlough, etc., was common in mission organisations at this time and continues to this day.

After World War II, many dependent nations began pressing for and gaining their independence from their colonisers. Dana Robert observes how 'many newly independent nations viewed Christianity as a Western religion closely identified with colonialism. Therefore, when they escaped the control of colonialism, they sought to limit the influence of Christianity as well.'[71] The

---

[66] Brian Stanley, *Christianity in the Twentieth Century: A World History* (Princeton: Princeton University Press, 2018), 196.

[67] Smither, 151.

[68] William Svelmoe, *A New Vision for Missions* (Tuscaloosa: University of Alabama Press, 2008), 18.

[69] Stanley, 196.

[70] David Kerr, and Kenneth Ross, *Edinburgh 2010: Mission Then and Now* (Oxford: Regnum, 2009), 3.

[71] Terry, and Gallagher, 279.

collapse of the European empires gave rise to the postcolonial-post imperialist period and a significant loss of influence of colonialism and, therefore, the control and exploitation of colonised people and their lands.

Historian Brian Stanley noted that the end of the twentieth century saw many Western church mainstream denominations 'confronted with the stark evidence of plummeting membership rolls and a critical paucity of recruits to the ordained ministry'. Many became open to 'accept that evangelism must form at least part of the core of the mission of the church', since the pressures of social justice had been leading some within the church to focus on social needs to the point of excluding evangelism.[72] At the same time, theologically conservative Christians 'no longer needed convincing that the gospel of the kingdom of God, which Jesus came to proclaim, must include an insistence on the social values of the kingdom and hence on the priority of justice. Christian mission would never be quite the same again.'[73]

By the end of the twentieth century, most Christians lived outside the West. Philip Jenkins notes, 'the era of Western Christianity has passed within our lifetime, and the day of Southern Christianity is dawning'.[74] In the twentieth century, 'Christianity became more truly a world religion than ever before'.[75] It was 'the century of the Bible' because 'more peoples received the Scriptures in their own languages than in any preceding century'.[76] This was also the century when many Christians identified themselves as having the responsibility of completing the Great Commission.[77]

Billy Graham initiated the Lausanne Congress for World Evangelization in 1974 (Lausanne I), bringing together leaders of 150 nations and showing how Christianity's shift to the Majority World was well underway. Noteworthy presenters included Ralph Winter, who expressed that 'unreached people groups should be given priority in mission' and René Padilla and Samuel Escobar, who called for 'a more holistic approach to mission'.[78] The resulting *Lausanne Covenant* set a course for the global evangelical theology of mission for the future.

In 1976, Winter established the US Center for World Mission in Pasadena, California. He brought attention to what he called 'the key to completing the Great Commission', shifting the focus from reaching countries to 'engaging people groups'.[79] Using texts such as Genesis 12:1-2 and the mention of 'families of the earth' and Matthew 28:18-20 and 'nations', Winter exegeted this to mean 'ethno-linguistic peoples' whom he defined as a 'grouping of individuals who

---

[72] Stanley, 214.

[73] Stanley, 214.

[74] Philip Jenkins, *The Next Christendom*, 3rd ed. (New York: Oxford University Press, 2011), 8.

[75] Stanley, 11.

[76] Stanley, 9.

[77] Charles Gailey, and Howard Culbertson, *Discovering Missions* (Kansas City: Beacon Hill Press, 2007), 14.

[78] Smither, 174.

[79] Smither, 168.

perceive themselves to have a common affinity with one another'.[80] Reaching these groups with the gospel could mean a church planting movement might be more readily established.

COMIBAM (Cooperación Misionera Iberoamericana)'s first Iberoamerica Mission Conference was held in São Paulo in 1987 and focused on world mission. More than 3,000 evangelical leaders from Latin America gathered, confirming what conference organisers hoped. 'The delegates affirmed that Latin America was becoming an active participant in world missions.'[81]

Lausanne II, held in Manila in 1989, included momentum to build upon Winter's people-group emphasis. For example, Luis Bush led an effort to focus on the unreached people groups who lived primarily in the '10/40 window' – the region between 10- and 40-degrees latitude between North Africa and Asia.

Late 1989 saw a sequence of 'popular revolutions in Eastern Europe that terminated the communist regimes of Poland, Hungary, East Germany, Bulgaria, Czechoslovakia, and Romania, and formed the writing on the wall for the survival of the Soviet Union, which finally broke up in December 1991'.[82] The churches in these lands now had greater freedom to participate in worldwide mission.

(2) Nationalism and postcolonialism in mission

Apartheid became official in South Africa in 1948 when the Nationalist Party created the policy accepted by the majority of 'Afrikaans-speaking white Christians as the only realistic solution to the problem of racial conflict [but it was] rejected by most other Christians as discriminatory and unjust'.[83] This political system was developed to 'safeguard the privileges of a minority white community against the black majority in the country'.[84] Apartheid affected many of the nation's white churches, often seen as part of the problem because they did not speak out against the policy. There were individual church leaders who led the stand against the injustices. A group of influential and mainly black South African theologians issued the Kairos Document of 1985 that highlighted the injustices of the system and gave a call to action. By the mid-1980s, South Africa had been affected by regional violence in protest of apartheid. The government declared a state of emergency that empowered the police to quell riots in black townships. This caught the world's attention. Greater pressure was placed on the government to dismantle this unjust system. Apartheid finally came to an end in the early 1990s through actions that led to creating a democratic government in 1994.

---

[80] Smither, 168.

[81] Todd Hartch, *The Rebirth of Latin American Christianity* (Oxford: Oxford University Press, 2014), 186.

[82] Stanley, 218.

[83] Kevin Roy, "South Africa," in *Evangelical Dictionary of World Missions*, ed. Scott Moreau (Grand Rapids: Baker Books, 2000), 898.

[84] G. Jan van Butselaar, "The Role of Churches in the Peace Process in Africa," in *The Changing Face of Christianity: Africa, the West, and the World*, ed. Lamin Sanneh and Joel Carpenter (Oxford: Oxford University Press, 2005), 108.

Dana Robert observes, 'During the 1960s, the voices of young nationalists grew louder in regional and international church councils, and they accused missionaries of paternalism and failing to turn over church leadership structures to national control quickly enough.'[85] These and other factors influenced a call for a moratorium on foreign missionary efforts in and to Africa.

In 1971, the Kenyan John Gatũ, serving as general secretary of the Presbyterian Church of East Africa, called for changes to how Western missions and the churches they started were conducting ministry in Africa. At a conference in New York, he stated, 'We cannot build the church in Africa on alms given by overseas churches; we are not serving the cause of the kingdom by turning all bishops, general secretaries, moderators, presidents, and superintendents into good, enthusiastic beggars when we continuously sing the tune of poverty in Third World churches.'[86] Gatũ championed 'principles of selfhood, self-reliance, and self-determination for the church and the nations of Africa', which became known worldwide as the Moratorium Debate. Later in his life, Gatũ observed how 'the call for a moratorium on missionaries... helped some missionary agencies re-examine their relevance in the changing world'.[87] He looked back on how many African leaders had been appointed to leadership roles with overseas mission organisations but managed to keep close links with their Western headquarters, returning there regularly to raise funds for the African work.

Liberian Canon Burgess Carr, a leading figure in the debate, attended the 1974 All Africa Conference of Churches (AACC), where the moratorium was discussed. The issue in focus was the African church's ability to 'speedily [move] towards achieving self-reliance'.[88] In Africa, there were some concerning challenges with foreign missionaries. Carr called this 'exploitative aspects of the modern missionary enterprise [where a] considerable portion of the money allocated for "missionary work" by missionary-sending agencies [was] spent on the salaries and maintenance of their own personnel'.[89] Carr concluded that after 'a hundred years of missionary activity in Africa, the Churches are still not able to *stand on their own feet*'.[90]

Later in 1974, Gatũ held a press briefing that coincided with the International Congress on World Evangelization at Lausanne, where the relationship between receiving and sending churches was discussed. Michael Cassidy outlines the four issues Gatũ presented:

> (1) the uncertain relationship that exists between the sending and receiving churches; (2) the need for selfhood and self-reliance of the church that has emerged on the mission field; (3) the need for the national church to take responsibility for mission with its own resources and people; and (4) the problem of institutions on

---

[85] Robert, 68.

[86] John Gatũ, *Fan into Flame: An Autobiography* (Nairobi: Moran Publishers, 2016), 128.

[87] Gatũ, 129.

[88] Burgess Carr, "The Engagement of Lusaka," *Pro Veritate* (June 1974): 8.

[89] Carr, 8.

[90] Carr, 8.

the mission field – those that may or may not be desired by the church, the supervision of such institutions, and resources to sustain them.[91]

Dana Robert also observes that 'in the early 1970s, leaders of Christian Councils in the South Pacific, South Asia, Latin America, and Africa called for a "moratorium" on the sending of foreign missionaries so they could break long-term patterns of dependency that had been established during the colonial era'.[92]

(3) Globalisation's early influences on mission

During the 1990s, globalisation was increasingly influencing worldwide events. Anthony Giddens defined globalisation as 'the intensification of worldwide social relations that link distant communities in such a way that local happenings are shaped by events occurring many miles away and vice versa'.[93] No longer were situations easily isolated from the rest of the world. These were the closing years of the Industrial Revolution. Globalisation was coming into prominence as multinational companies were able to develop global workforces and markets. The global economic engine opened up new trade relationships, fuelled by goods being moved cheaply and quickly across the world, the growing presence of global banks, and progressive governments removing financial barriers. News, ideologies, influence, and developments were able to spread more quickly. Technology was increasing, impacting all areas of life, particularly communication.

The Union of Soviet Socialist Republics (USSR) collapsed in 1991. The interconnection of communication and globalisation meant the rest of the world quickly witnessed the unfolding event. This downfall ended the bipolar world of the USSR bloc and US bloc, which had been in a lengthy political, military, and socio-economic stand-off known as the Cold War since around 1950. Quickly, with the void left by the demise of the USSR, the US became regarded as the dominant world power. Freedom from tyranny was a value that the US and its Western friends now wanted to promote across the world as a form of neo-colonialism. There was a biblical basis amongst US Christians who believed that 'everybody wants to be free, politically and economically; God made human beings with the desire to be free'.[94]

Summary

In this chapter, we reviewed the journey of where we have come from. We followed David Bosch's framing of church and mission history in six paradigms, starting with the New Testament church and ending with the ecumenical

---

[91] Michael Cassidy, "The Call to Moratorium: Perspective on an Identity Crisis," *Churchman* 90, no. 4 (1976): 267, accessed 29 August 2020, https://churchsociety.org/docs/churchman/090/Cman_090_4_Cassidy.pdf.
[92] Robert, 68.
[93] Anthony Giddens, *The Third Way* (Cambridge: Polity Press, 1998), 64.
[94] Nicholas Wolterstorff, "Foreword," in *Evangelicals and Empire: Christian Alternatives to the Political Status Quo*, ed. Bruce Benson and Peter Heltzel (Grand Rapids: Brazos Press, 2008), 7.

paradigm of the early twentieth century. Through this exploration, we saw how most of these paradigms and their shifts took time. Within each paradigm were specific theological, missiological, and cultural elements at play.

Many implications still influence mission today. Here are three: (1) Christendom was birthed in the mid-fourth century with Constantine's conversion and his co-opting of Christianity as the state religion. This meant the church moved from the margins to a place of privilege, material wealth, territory, and power. (2) Spanish and Portuguese colonial expansion into the New World in the sixteenth century extended the existing model, where the church and territory were considered synonymous. The pope sanctioned conquest on the condition that those conquered convert to Christianity. (3) The Reformation did not significantly alter the dynamic of mission. Protestants were slow to engage in mission. One reason why Roman Catholics dismissed Protestants as not being Christian was that they did not engage in mission. However, the development of colonial power and the migration of Europeans (50 million) in the late eighteenth through the nineteenth and early twentieth centuries facilitated the development of the Protestant mission movement.

We can conclude from this review of the six paradigm shifts that the history of the expansion of Christianity is both inspiring and terrifying.

Reflective Questions:

> - What key lessons can you apply from each of the six eras covered in this sweep of the past 2,000 years of Christian mission?
> - In your opinion, which of the past influences upon mission are evident in the six paradigms that still affect how mission is understood and practised today?

3. Christendom Mission

Introduction

Now we will examine our current understanding of mission by observing the paradigm of Christendom's development and ongoing influence upon mission today.

Our interest in church and mission history is because 'history repeats itself. It has to; nobody listens the first time around.' This paraphrase originates from Spanish philosopher George Santayana's quote: 'Those who cannot learn from history are doomed to repeat it.'[1] This reminds us of the value of historical studies. In his *Historical Theology*, Alister McGrath states that 'history makes us alert to both the mistakes of the past and the alarming way in which they are repeated in the present'.[2] John Johnson makes a compelling case for why this is important: 'Every person and every organisation has a history, and it needs careful attention. People need to read their ancestors, and organizations need to read their pasts.'[3] Learning from mission history captures the faith and vision of ancestors and their organisations of the recent past. Johnson also observes how people, especially leaders, tend to 'ignore the past' because they want to 'scrap what's in place and charge into the future'.[4]

Overview of Christendom

The Christendom paradigm has had the most significant influence on modern Western missions. Carrying a narrower meaning than the term 'Christianity', Christendom began and grew out of Western Christianity as it moved from the margins in the fourth century and became part of established religion when Emperor Constantine adopted Christianity as the state religion. As Christianity began to hold a position of power in Western Europe, it became linked to political and military power. Historically, Christendom has been recognised and rooted in the identity it gave its members. Jehu Hanciles describes it this way:

> To be a member of society was to be a Christian, to be a Christian was to be a member of society. Christendom represented Christianity as tribal religion. The introduction and spread of feudal social structure with an emphasis on reciprocal

---

[1] "George Santayana," accessed 30 May 2022, https://en.wikiquote.org/wiki/George_Santayana.

[2] Alister McGrath, *Historical Theology: An Introduction to the History of Christian Thought*, 2nd ed. (Oxford: Wiley, 2013), 14.

[3] John Johnson, *Missing Voices: Learning to Lead Beyond Our Horizons* (Carlisle: Langham Global Library, 2019), 239.

[4] Johnson, 239.

obligations and binding oaths further strengthened the process: religious allegiance, already inseparable from tribal identity, became fused with political loyalty.[5]

Christianity began to manifest domination over all relationships and allegiances. To be part of Christendom was not necessarily based on personal faith in Christ but a consequence of belonging to a Christian denomination or nation. Throughout the world and throughout history, popular definitions of Christendom include the worldwide body or society of those who call themselves Christians and the collective body of those claiming to be Christians.[6]

The term Christendom was used extensively in the 1850s and for about 100 years, peaking in the post-1910 era. More recently, it enjoyed a resurgence around 2010, likely because of the global Christian mission conferences Edinburgh 2010, Cape Town 2010, 2010Boston,[7] and Tokyo 2010.

The term Christendom expresses both the popular view of Christianity as a whole, as well as the more nuanced view of Christianity attached to political and economic power. For example:

• Western European Christianity, commencing with Roman emperor Constantine's incredible support of the church, with special imperial favours and status; and

• A description of any place where 'Christian forms and structures are firmly entrenched within a society'.[8] When Phillip Jenkins describes the church in the Global South – now reaching a point in several nations where it completely dominates the religious sphere – he is describing the next Christendom.

Through the lens of paradigm theory, the paradigm of Christendom includes its core beliefs, values, rules, and guidelines expressed and followed within its worldwide community, which we will explore below. This paradigm was centuries in the making, as we have seen, dating from the fourth century. Over time, the worldview of Christendom has greatly influenced the Christian church in mission.

Characteristics of Christendom Mission

Alan and Eleanor Kreider summarise the Protestant cross-cultural missionary movement based on a Christendom worldview as presenting four key elements which characterised mission values in the nineteenth and twentieth centuries.[9]

---

[5] Hanciles, 84–85.

[6] Dictionary.com summarises this as: 'Christians collectively', 'the Christian world', and 'Christianity', accessed 30 June 2022, https://www.dictionary.com/browse/christendom.

[7] Allen Yeh states: 'it was called "2010Boston" instead of "Boston 2010" in order to emphasize the year instead of the city', Allen Yeh, *Polycentric Missiology: Twenty-First Century Mission from Everyone to Everywhere* (Downers Grove: IVP Academic, 2016), 162.

[8] Hanciles, 85.

[9] Alan Kreider, and Eleanor Kreider, *Worship and Mission After Christendom* (Milton Keynes: Paternoster, 2009), 37–38.

These elements continue to influence how mission is perceived, not necessarily arising from or reflecting on Scripture in our current context but from the assumptions and baggage that have come out of this Western Christendom context.

(1) Territory defined the sphere of mission: Christendom mission referred to a world divided between Christian and non-Christian territories. Mission is inevitably linked to sending when viewed from a Christendom model in territorial terms, though we will observe that mission in this sense has not always occurred this way in church history.

Recognising that mission now emerges from every continent to every continent, this still defines mission in terms of sending, which remains the prevalent mindset. Cross-cultural workers can attest to it being easier to raise financial support when serving overseas than in the home country.

(2) The sender is the church: The question arises as to who the owner and driver of mission is. The Christendom model saw mission as primarily the church's responsibility, with the goal of expansion of the church. Selective use of biblical texts such as Matthew 28:18-20, John 20:21, and Acts 1:8 has been considered the primary lens through which mission is observed and known. The language used, such as 'finish the task', suggests that the church is responsible for mission. When mission is exclusively predicated on the command to go, that immediately assumes that the church is required to carry out mission; that mission is its responsibility. While some elements of that are relevant, such as our obedience to the command of Christ, it is not the whole story.

(3) Agents are a professional mission cadre: Mission, linked with a territorial conception, requires specialists called missionaries, set aside to accomplish the mission task. In contrast with the early centuries of the church, when reviewing the Protestant missionary movement of the eighteenth, nineteenth, and early twentieth centuries, Andrew Walls comments that 'full commitment to the cause of missions was in practice always an elite movement'.[10] It is worth noting that missionary elitism, at least in the US, began to wane after World War II. The notion was that anyone could be a missionary, without any particular skill or background. Nonetheless, mission as cross-cultural sending remained an elite movement in the sense that not all members of the church could participate in it. In general, missionaries were separated from the rest of the church for this function. Very few people in Christendom could participate in mission. One of the continuing and significant complications of equating mission with sending is that most Christians are excluded or have excluded themselves from participation in God's mission by the narrowly defined terms 'mission' and 'missionary'.

4) The goal of mission was the expansion of the church: The ultimate goal of mission was the expansion of the church, typically in a form indistinguishable from the sending context. It was difficult for those going overseas to separate their experience of the church – which reflected centuries of a Christendom

---

[10] Andrew Walls, *The Cross-Cultural Process in Christian History* (Maryknoll: Orbis Books, 2017), 219.

context – from what they sought to plant; however, this did not mean that mission was reductionist, comprising solely evangelism and church planting. Although a Christendom interpretation of the goal of mission was the establishment of the church, that doesn't mean that those involved in cross-cultural ministry had a narrow view of their involvement in other areas. For example, Robert Woodberry notes how many Protestant missionaries in the nineteenth and early part of the twentieth centuries 'were a crucial catalyst initiating the development and spread of religious liberty, mass education, newspapers, voluntary organizations, most major colonial reforms, and the codification of legal protections for non-whites'.[11] However, some ways of organising and engaging in church activity – such as worship style, church structures, and even wearing woollen cassocks in tropical countries – were merely recasting what was adopted from the home country experience and imposing on the new setting. While missionaries generally saw their main objective as planting and reproducing churches, they recognised that the church's mission was more than just winning others to Christ and discipling them into worshipping communities. It's one thing to say that is the heart of mission; it's another thing to say it is the goal of mission. The Scriptures point to the larger goal in God's purposes, in which we participate through mission.

The Kreider's approach to the Christendom paradigm of mission sees it as territorial, the work and responsibility of the church, requiring specialist workers, and with the goal of church planting. These four criteria arose out of a context of mission. However, the prevailing Christendom approach to mission made little sense to many Christian leaders from the Majority World at the 1974 Lausanne Conference. They were determined to have a different understanding of mission that was integral or holistic. This led to sharp disagreement between some Majority World and Western leaders.

The church of Christendom still exists in a place of power – socially, economically, and politically – though greater awareness of the concerns that these issues bring to mission has occurred in the West in the second half of the twentieth century. More importantly, the Christendom concepts and ideas that defined mission continue, even if modified, in mission thinking. Territory – the idea of some places being Christian and others not – has been replaced by ethnicity. Some ethnic groups need mission, and others do not. For example, mission strategists may define that need as less than 2% of a society involved and engaged in the church. Thus, ethnicity becomes the definer today, as territory was before. However, who determines which ethnic groups and what percentages indicate a need for mission is a complex issue.

The Christendom paradigm continues to influence how mission is perceived today. These four characteristics provide an important background to defining a course for mission in the global church of the twenty-first century.

---

[11] Robert D. Woodberry, "The Missionary Roots of Liberal Democracy," *American Political Science Review* 106, no. 2 (2012): 244–45, https://dx.doi.org/10.1017/S0003055412000093.

Modern Mission Era (Twentieth to early Twenty-First Centuries)

We start with Kreider's four marks to see how the Christendom paradigm of mission has shifted to what they call the *missio Dei* paradigm: 'Mission after Christendom'.[12]

(1) Territory was in focus primarily for Western missionaries who were 'sent abroad "out there," to "regions beyond" Christendom, to heathendom'.[13] This changed to an awareness that in the *missio Dei*, God is already at work everywhere and potentially in all kinds of people. Samuel Escobar popularised this shift in the title of his book *The New Global Mission: The Gospel from Everywhere to Everyone.*[14]

(2) The sender was the church in Christendom, supported by selective Great Commission texts. In the new paradigm, 'the sender is God'.[15] He initiates his mission and invites collaboration from all kinds of people, regardless of whether they are called 'missionaries', but, importantly, those who are led and empowered by the Holy Spirit for effectiveness in God's mission.

(3) Agents in Christendom were exceptional people, set aside to serve in ecclesiastical roles as full-time Christian workers. In the shift, this changed to include all Christians whom God sends to be the agents of his mission.

(4) The goal of Christendom's mission was the expansion of the church through planting and reproducing churches. Under *missio Dei*, it became much larger. While it included individual salvation through evangelism and church reproduction, mission came to embrace the fullness of salvation that includes *shalom* and abundant life in the kingdom of God.

One wonders whether we have fully shifted to the *missio Dei* paradigm. However, paradigm shifts are messy and therefore, the Christendom paradigm still influences us today. For example, mission may still be considered something the church fulfils through mission organisations, denominations, or others. Missionaries, especially cross-cultural ones, may still be viewed as elite. Mission may still be viewed narrowly as just church planting.

We have thought earlier about how paradigms begin to change when they no longer make sense of reality. The Christendom paradigm of mission started to be severely tested for several reasons, including the following:

- The continued demographic shift in Christianity, with the decline of the Western church and growth in the churches in the Majority World.

- The continued rise of secular materialism.

- The rise of postcolonial studies of the cultural legacy of colonialism and its consequences on colonised people and their lands, fostering a growing awareness of how colonialism has impacted mission.

A factor affecting this era is the legacy of North America's influence of pragmatism on mission. This involves using whatever means worked to achieve

---

[12] Kreider, and Kreider, 43.
[13] Kreider, and Kreider, 50.
[14] Samuel Escobar, *The New Global Mission: The Gospel from Everywhere to Everyone* (Downers Grove: InterVarsity Press, 2003).
[15] Kreider, and Kreider, 49.

an outcome. An example among evangelicals in the late twentieth century was their extraordinary and singular focus on methods to ensure the church's numerical growth. Were we to study pragmatism in mission through the lens of Mission Theology, we would need to consider biblical texts, mission history, anthropology, and other disciplines to discover the reason for this approach, its merits, and the concerns to be addressed.

Researcher of world Christianity Gina Zurlo states: 'Christianity is the world's largest religion; with over 2.5 billion members, it comprises 32% of the world's global population.'[16] This 'has dropped slightly over the last 120 years [from] 34% of the world's population in 1900 [to] 32% in 2020. However, the world Christian movement grew from 558 million to 2.5 billion, with most of that growth occurring in the global South [or Majority World]'.[17] Despite the decline of the church in the West and the rise of secular materialism, the number of evangelical Protestant mission agencies mushroomed during this era. Many focused on specific kinds of ministry or groups of people, such as unreached people groups. Strategy, speed, and scale became significant drivers. Demographics have shifted to more than 60% of global Christianity being located outside the context where the Christendom model of mission originated. The contexts of Latin America, Africa, and parts of Asia are very different from that Christendom context.

Despite these challenges to the Christendom mission model, it has continued to strongly influence the evangelical Protestant mission mindset, perpetuating a power imbalance within the global cross-cultural mission movement, evidenced in the influence of Western mission activity across the globe. Consciously or unconsciously, a dynamic existed in which the mission movement and its supporters held power (financial, educational, cultural, etc.), influencing the way assumptions and beliefs are shaped in relationships with the emerging churches of the South. The power dynamic reflected both current and historical realities. The efforts of Christian mission spread to every part of the world, and churches were established. This form of mission was birthed in Christian Europe and was reflected in European migration, colonialism, and a call to civilise the world. Consequently, new mission movements from the Majority World have been brought largely uncritically into Christendom's model for mission, even though it was inappropriate to expect them to fit within this earlier model.

By the 1990s, mission efforts had introduced the gospel to '58 percent of the world's people groups, especially the larger, more populous groups'.[18] However, this was not enough. Luis Bush and Thomas Wang started the AD2000 movement, endeavouring to evangelise 'all peoples' by the year 2000. As noted earlier, Bush believed a movement was the best way to do this because it is 'a place to foment harmony, common purpose, innovation, and renewal'.[19] The goal

---

[16] Zurlo, 3.

[17] Zurlo, 4.

[18] Terry, and Gallagher, 297.

[19] Luis Bush, "AD2000 and Beyond: Toward a Conceptual Model," in *Working Together With God to Shape the New Milliennium: Opportunities & Limitations*, ed. Gary Corwin and Kenneth Mulholland (Pasadena: William Carey Library, 2000), 197.

of this movement was 'all the gospel to all peoples in all places by the Church – Christ's Kingdom Come'.[20]

The Christendom mission paradigm, focused on sending and arising from a particular history and context, has at times demonstrated an ignorance of the church's existence in every nation in proximity to those groups and communities without visible witness to Christ. This 'local' church has access to all peoples, nations, tribes, and languages, yet the supposition that the primary agent of mission must be one sent from a distance risks obscuring the likelihood that God is using local Christians to grow the church and to be a witness to Christ. Furthermore, church growth has always happened primarily when local Christians have taken the initiative to reach out and live out their faith.

Hostility towards the church in the West has become more overt, making it necessary for the Western church to learn to live as the people of God and be a blessing in exile as pilgrim people in their part of the world that is becoming post-Christian.[21] This reality is contributing to re-evaluation and reframing of mission by many in the West.

After 1,000 years of largely Western prominence in Christendom and 200 years of Western leadership in the modern mission movement, there is now a seismic shift taking place thanks to the growth of the global church and the growing representation of voices, especially from the Majority World.

Post-Christendom Mission (Early Twenty-First Century)

As we move deeper into the current era and the emerging paradigm of global Christianity, it is essential to consider the changes occurring in mission contexts. In the past, mission endeavours focused on issues of geography and ethnicity, such as unreached people groups. Increasingly, the mission movement requires a focus on other critical frontiers of post-Christendom.[22]

In his book *Mission after Christendom,* David Smith identified secularisation, pluralisation, and globalisation as the leading issues confronting the church in mission.[23] With these in mind, the language and methodology of mission arising out of Christendom will be increasingly inadequate in promoting mutual participation. A further look at some issues for mission in the era of global Christianity provides insights into paradigm shifts taking place and giving rise to other mission models.

(1) Globalisation: This multidimensional social process and interconnection increase and intensify social interactions, linking them together so that local developments in one part of the world are affected by events in other regions. This is enabled by broad changes in economic activity and scope that bring

---

[20] Bush, 199.

[21] James Davison Hunter, *To Change the World: The Irony, Tragedy, and Possibility of Christianity in the Late Modern World* (New York: Oxford University Press, 2011), 275.

[22] Hunter, 275.

[23] David Smith, *Mission After Christendom* (London: Darton, Longman and Todd Ltd, 2003).

together information and knowledge from all parts of the world so that, theoretically, more of humanity can participate in the free flow of trade, capital, information, and labour across borders. As a result, location is not the principal factor, and people of all nations and cultural contexts can participate. It is an interconnected world made possible through widespread access to innovative and converging technologies, combined with economic and political influences, to produce dynamic forces not bound to a particular geographic or cultural context. Christianity is both an agent and a product of globalisation as its beliefs have spread from one source to another, crossing numerous religious, linguistic, and cultural contexts, giving Christians a sense of identity, connection, and belonging to a global body of believers. However, the converse is also true. Globalisation enables communities to have a sociopolitical, socio-economic, or political identity without any link to a religious identity. Other forces are on the rise that are a reaction to globalisation, such as nationalism, the protection of local markets, anti-migration, and xenophobia. Time will tell to what degree these forces will limit globalisation and in what ways they will affect the church and its practice of mission.

(2) Worldview and religious frontiers: When considering the world religions of Islam, Buddhism, and Hinduism, we need to do so with care because all are highly complex and diverse contexts. We risk reducing great diversity into simple monolithic 'blocks' that we can 'master'. One of the dangers of focusing on religious frontiers (the boundaries between different belief systems) is that too narrow a view may hinder our understanding of the other frontiers (or extreme limits) immediately around us, such as non-religious worldviews of secular humanism and materialism. Both present themselves as significant frontiers for the gospel today and are increasingly present alongside each other. This complexity requires more mission scholarship to help understand and deal with the challenges they raise. A worldview of secular materialism, though prevalent in the West, has penetrated large sections of the world, including those religious 'blocks' (a region where a world religion is the majority occupant). For example, the church in Tunisia has grown slowly. Why is that? Tunisia has a relatively moderate and open form of Islam, and Christians are not generally persecuted, even those who originate in an Islamic context. Why has the church struggled so much to grow? Tunisia has developed over the last 50 to 60 years, with up to 70% of the population counted as middle class. A fusion between secular humanism and Islam has occurred. On the surface, people announce allegiance to Islam when, in fact, their worldview is also shaped by materialism, presenting perhaps the most challenging religious worldview to encounter.

(3) Urban mission: Due to globalisation, the search for economic progress and prosperity, and the rapid pace of urbanisation, 55% of the world's population now lives in cities compared to less than 10% in 1800.[24] This migration from rural areas to urban areas has contributed to the development of mega-cities of up to ten million people and meta-cities and super-cities that are 'massive

---

[24] "Urbanization," accessed 30 April 2023,
https://ourworldindata.org/urbanization#number-of-people-living-in-urban-areas.

sprawling [metropolises] of more than 20 million people'.[25] By 2050, there will be an estimated 23 meta-cities, with the ten largest in Asia and Africa.

The world's great global cities (e.g. London, Beijing, Tokyo, New York, Hong Kong) have more influence over the global context than do many nation-states. Not only is there a massive population density, but enormous financial, spiritual, and cultural influence as well. Because of their great diversity and financial, transportation, and economic connections globally, cities like New York and Hong Kong are a microcosm of globalisation. Globalisation and pluralism, plus immigration, have created a context of hybridity and multiculturalism in prominent cities. There is no longer a dominant culture. Global cities provide meeting grounds for people of all cultures, religions, and worldviews. Though all these factors are acknowledged, there is still little research into how urban mission functions in these contexts.

(4) Migration and hybridity: Human migration has played a significant role in the spread of Christianity. It is not a new phenomenon either. Migration, according to Jehu Hanciles, is in *'constant change, marked by varying degrees of compulsion (or freedom), and shaped by wider structures and historical processes.'*[26] Voluntary migration is not the same as diaspora, cautions Willie James Jennings, 'because diaspora is a geographic and social world not chosen and a psychic state inescapable'.[27] The intermixing of people and their cultures as they relocate produces 'something new'.[28] The movement of people means they 'enter new spheres which they have to negotiate and navigate. As they move and mix, they spawn hybridization and are themselves hybridized'.[29]

Harvey Kwiyani notes how 'cultural diversity, resulting from the shrinking global village and the migration of millions of non-Western Christians to the West', is already impacting the 'Western religious and cultural landscape of the twenty-first century'.[30] This is likened to the reversal of European migration of previous eras. Consequently, 'people can no longer be defined geographically'.[31] Sam George notes how 'Non-Western missionaries are relocating in obedience to the mission call from the Scripture and employing every viable means, including migration (for education, work, business, and safety)'.[32]

---

[25] United Nations, *Urbanization: Mega & Meta Cities, New City States* (New York: United Nations, 2006).

[26] Hanciles, 19. Emphasis original.

[27] Jennings, 6.

[28] Harvey C. Kwiyani, "Diaspora, Hybridity and Theology," in *A Hybrid World: Diaspora, Hybridity, and Missio Dei*, ed. Sadiri Joy Tira and Juliet Lee Uytanlet (Littleton: William Carey Publishing, 2020), 47.

[29] Calvin Chong, "Globalization, Hybrid Worlds, and Emerging Missional Frontiers," in *A Hybrid World: Diaspora, Hybridity, and Missio Dei*, 71.

[30] Harvey C. Kwiyani, *Multicultural Kingdom: Ethnic Diversity, Mission and the Church* (London: SCM Press, 2020), 14.

[31] Sam George, "Reimagining Go and Send Mission Paradigms for an Age of Global Migration and World Christianity," *International Bulletin of Mission Research* 47, no. 2 (2023): 254, https://dx.doi.org/10.1177/239639393221120499.

[32] George, 256.

Migration into urban areas creates pluralistic environments from multicultural and multireligious situations. Migration, diaspora, displacement, and hybridisation issues related to urbanisation and globalisation require further investigation to determine mission approaches. The reality of this vast mission frontier calls for additional reflection.

(5) Frontiers of postmodernity: These are extensive and impacted by today's fast-paced change. Postmodernism implies a break with modernism. Modernism was 'a manifesto of human self-confidence and self-congratulation; postmodernism is a confession of modesty, if not despair'.[33] However, as postmodernism progresses, while there is despair, there is little modesty. As various groups see new opportunities to be privileged, they grasp supposed power. At the other extreme, groups display inflated senses of self, claiming responsibility for history, events, and conditions in which they may have had some impact but nothing like what they claim. Nor is there anything modest about claiming everyone has their own truth. Our sinful nature doesn't allow for modesty.

Postmodernity's version of truth is viewed as subjective, as freedom of choice. According to Knud Jørgensen, any choice of values may be of equal validity because, 'there is no truth, only truths. Principles are replaced by preferences. Instead of grand reason, we have only reasons'.[34] This relativism, which is 'any theory holding that criteria of judgment are relative, varying with individuals and their environments',[35] encourages freedom to choose one's truth. 'In a postmodern perspective, these Enlightenment values [e.g. modernism, reason, and rationality] come to be seen as… just one tradition among others; it is up to the individual to shop around for the values they prefer.'[36] Jørgensen further notes, 'There is no privileged civilization or culture or belief, only a multiplicity of cultures and beliefs. The grand narrative of human progress of modernity has been transformed into the numerous small stories of peoples and cultures.'[37]

Postmodernism moves from realism to the social construction of reality and, as Stanley Grentz observes, 'from metanarrative to local stories'.[38] A *metanarrative* is a narrative or story about narratives of historical meaning,

---

[33] Os Guinness, *Fit Bodies, Fat Minds: Why Evangelicals Don't Think, and What to Do About It* (Grand Rapids: Baker, 1994), 103–105.

[34] Knud Jørgensen, "Foreword," in *Mission and Postmodernities*, ed. Rolv Olsen (Oxford: Regnum Books International, 2011), viii.

[35] 'Relativism', accessed 10 January 2019, from https://www.dictionary.com/browse/relativism?s=t.

[36] Richard Bauckman, "Bible and Mission: The Modern/Postmodern Western Context," in Pauline Hoggarth et al., *Bible in Mission*, ed. Pauline Hoggarth (Oxford: Regnum, 2013), 52.

[37] Jørgensen, in *Mission and Postmodernities*, viii.

[38] D.A. Carson, "Domesticating the Gospel: A Review of Grenz's Renewing the Center," in *Reclaiming the Center: Confronting Evangelical Accommodation: In Postmodern Times*, ed. Millard J. Erickson, Paul Kjoss Helseth, and Justin Taylor (Wheaton: Crossway, 2004), 35.

experience, or knowledge which offers a society legitimation through the anticipated completion of an as yet unrealised master plan. The biblical metanarrative traces the storyline of the Bible from Genesis to Revelation. It is the triumphant story of God ruling as king over his realm. He does so for his own glory in an all-out war with Satan and his rival kingdom of evil. The biblical narrative includes a fundamental understanding of what it means to be human and all the ethical issues related to that: human sexuality, gender fluidity, genetic manipulation, and control of life and death.

In the communications arena, we see the growing interrelationship with technology, artificial intelligence, social media, mass media, journalism, film, and virtual relationships, impacting our perception of who we are as human beings and how we live in society. We see the challenge of what Gregg Okesson calls the 'thick webs of public life', where thickness refers to the depth and complexity of life in society.[39] This very depth may hinder the ability of Christians to effectively communicate their message to the public if they have been conditioned to think of the gospel in simplistic terms, focusing solely on individual conversion. Salvation encompasses more than just individual transformation. Therefore, 'public missiology requires a robust understanding of salvation'.[40]

The church needs to consider how to engage more effectively in all these frontiers and the challenges they present. This involves taking the time to pause and reflect on God's missional response to these frontiers. It is a call to be reflective practitioners – someone who

> anchors his or her action and study upon the Bible, has an awareness of global realities and the church, and understands how to integrate these components into their response to God's invitation to join him in his mission. The reflective practitioner's goal is to demonstrate an integrated nature – action and study that is glocal and global, Christ-centred and biblical.[41]

Missio Dei After Christendom

The Christendom model – with its now seemingly simplistic views of sending, special agents, and the church with the goal of replication – will fail us if we continue to cling to it in the future. Earlier, we explored the theological development of *missio Dei* and how this was interpreted throughout recent church history. We gained insights into how these positions varied through time and were affected by various events and people. That exploration gives us lenses to view the changing mission paradigm after Christendom. This is of relevance, because we've come to realise that it is God's mission. God reveals himself as the one who loves the world; he is involved with and embraces the church and the world, highlighting our privileged participation in his mission.

---

[39] Gregg Okesson, *A Public Missiology: How Local Churches Witness to a Complex World* (Grand Rapids: Baker Academic, 2020), 23.
[40] Okesson, 23.
[41] Kirk Franklin, *Towards Global Missional Leadership* (Oxford: Regnum Books International, 2017), 95.

Bosch reminds us that paradigm shifts take time. As changes take place, we do not fully know what is emerging. But we can assert that ultimately, the outcome of mission is *shalom*, the redemption and renewal of the whole of creation – where the reign of God is fully restored, in which all things in heaven and earth find their place together under the Lordship of Jesus. Therefore, mission must involve the whole church, since the whole church is called to bear witness to God's purposes and activities, fulfilled in Jesus Christ. This contrasts with Christendom's mission, which focused on an identity based on institutions and nations. Whenever mission structures exist, they should facilitate the work of the whole church in mission and not operate separately from it. Our posture within God's mission includes wonder, worship, dependence, prayer, humility, and celebration.

Summary

Scott Sunquist observes, 'When Christianity entered the twentieth century, it was a confident, strong, imperial religion of the West.'[42] Fast forward to the end of the twentieth century, when 'religionists, the historians, and the politicians… were surprised' by the 'unexpected' Christian century of global mission.[43] The effects of a thousand years of Christendom have seen the Western form of Christianity lose its predominant place in global Christianity. The Western world, however, has led the modern missionary movement of the past 200 years. Therefore, intentional efforts are necessary to overcome the gaps between the Christendom paradigm and global church paradigm.

Through our exploration, we have seen how the Christian faith is not static. In terms of its growth, Andrew Walls observes that 'the nature of Christian expansion isn't progressive; it is serial'.[44] Consider places that were Christian long ago but may not be today. For example, places like Egypt, Syria, or Tunisia:

These were once the showcase churches that led the Christian world, adorned by the greatest theologians and the most profound scholars, and sanctified by the blood of the Martyrs. They were churches that had seen the collapse of paganism around them and the triumphs of Christ throughout their surrounding areas.[45]

The Christian faith doesn't conquer and hold territory very well. History shows us how growth is not guaranteed. We see this in how the strength and superior position of Christendom mission is now faltering.

---

[42] Sunquist, xvi.

[43] Sunquist, xvi.

[44] Andrew Walls, "Demographics, Power and the Gospel in the 21st Century" (paper presented to SIL International Conference and WBTI Convention, Waxhaw NC, US, 2002).

[45] Walls, 1.

Reflective Questions:

- What are some broad characteristics of the Christendom paradigm that you still see at work in the church and mission, locally, regionally, and globally?
- What are the differences and similarities between the Christendom paradigm and the *missio Dei* paradigm?

4. Mission in the Global Church

Introduction

As we journey deeper into the twenty-first century, we consider how mission will reflect the global church. This is affected in part because of the demographic shift that is decades in the making, most noticeable in the demographic growth of Christianity in Africa, Asia, and Latin America – the Majority World.

While many in the ecumenical movement predicted the demise of the modern mission movement, Dana Robert identified that 'the most significant development in the structure of missions was not the end of the missionary movement but its transformation into a multi-cultural, multi-faceted network'.[1] No clear signposts tell us what mission will become as it grapples with a movement birthed from Christendom and new concepts continue to arise. Rupen Das claims that the Majority World has 'a deep appreciation for what historical missions have contributed to the church and society'.[2] Since mission is not static, it is moving forward. This requires that we learn from the past, rely on God's leading, and seek to discern the times wisely.

The Global Church Paradigm

Edward Smither refers to this new era as 'Mission from the Majority World', but what to call this phenomenon has not been straightforward. So far, various other terms that describe the shift include 'Global South', 'non-Western', 'third-world', 'two-thirds world', and 'developing world' Christianity.[3] It is identified by various titles:

- the church of the southern continent;
- the church of the South and East;
- the church of the non-Western world;
- the church of the Majority World;[4]
- global Christianity;[5]
- world Christianity.[6]

---

[1] Robert, 73.

[2] Rupen Das, "What the Majority World Is Saying About Mission Today," *Evangelical Review of Theology* 46, no. 3 (2022): 199.

[3] Smither, 165.

[4] Lalsangkima Pachuau, *World Christianity: A Historical and Theological Introduction* (Nashville: Abingdon Press, 2018), 5.

[5] Douglas Jacobsen, *Global Gospel: An Introduction to Christianity on Five Continents* (Grand Rapids: Baker Academic, 2015), ix–x.

[6] Pachuau, 3.

The point is that a new descriptive term is needed because most of the world's Christians now reside in continents that were predominantly non-Christian during the nineteenth century.[7] The global church doesn't have a defined doctrine, geographic centre, or single dominant leader.[8] A result of the shift to the global church paradigm is 'new voices… waiting to be heard, and fresh formulations of Christian faith and life [that] are ready to be uncovered'.[9]

Characteristics of the Global Church

Since the paradigm is still emerging, we now consider some of its features.

(1) Multiethnic: The global church comes from various ethnic, cultural, national, and linguistic backgrounds. Approximately 67% of the world's Christian population resides in the Majority World, with the remaining 33% in the Western world. While Western Christianity has enormous diversity that has influenced the faith, this doesn't adequately describe the global Christian community's 'beliefs, values, practices, and affections'.[10]

Majority World missionaries from contexts like South Korea, Brazil, Nigeria, India, and the Philippines have increased in numbers. Their advantages include better access to restrictive countries, deeper understanding of hardship and suffering, and respect for cultural and spirit-world contexts. Similarities between their cultures and the cultures they hope to reach further enhance their effectiveness. However, they also face challenges of limited training, resources, missionary care, language barriers in partnering with the global North, instances of racism, and political obstacles.

Jay Matenga states that this new era includes the 'indigenous shift' with its own epistemé (knowledge and understanding).[11] This way of knowing or understanding is interconnected and spiritually aware, with relationships that 'are mutual, reciprocal, and familial'.[12] It holds a collectivist orientation where 'harmony and the interdependence of group members are stressed and valued'.[13] This is in contrast to individualistic societies where personal needs take precedence over those of the group.

(2) Multidirectional and polycentric: According to Sam George, mission is now 'from everywhere to everywhere, multilateral, multidirectional, sending as well as

---

[7] Pachuau, 3.

[8] Jacobsen, xv.

[9] Jacobsen, xvi.

[10] Jacobsen, xv.

[11] Jay Matenga, "A New Era of Missions" (paper presented at the Mission Interlink Conference, Melbourne, Australia, 2022).

[12] Matenga, 3.

[13] Craig Storti, *Figuring Foreigners Out: A Practical Guide* (Yarmouth: InterCultural Press, 1999), 25–26.

receiving'.[14] The concepts of 'multidirectional scattering and gathering'[15] serve as useful themes for understanding the current movement of God in the world.

The growing global church is also polycentric in nature, revealed by the gospel flowing in all directions. Through polycentrism, there is a deliberate movement away from established centres of power, so that influence occurs among and with others, while the community creatively learns together. To those used to having a measure of control and dominant influence, this may seem chaotic and uncoordinated. Polycentric mission can be conceptualised through Table 1.

Polycentric Mission (many aspects; many parts)	
Biblical Insights	**Concepts and Benefits**
Every tribe, language, people, nation (Rev. 5:9, 7:9)	A picture of multiple centres of influence
Paul's heritage (Jewish, Roman, Greek, Diaspora)	Advantage of hybridity and diversity
Churches established in variety of centres of influence (e.g. Jerusalem, Antioch, Corinth, Rome, Philippi, etc.)	Gospel spread through multiple centres of influence involving people and places from diversity of culture and worldviews
Each belongs to the other with different functions and giftings; all parts caring for each other (Rom. 12, 1 Cor. 12); each one does its part (Eph. 4:16); shared fellowship (1 John 1:3); serve one another (1 Pet. 4:10)	Multiple and different parts working together with diversity of functions and gifts of service for benefit of all
Encourage each other (Heb. 10:24); honouring one another (Rom. 12:10)	Christ connects the various parts; each part has a unique personality and gifting; community takes place for fellowship; a reality shared
Equally important and on the same team (1 Cor. 3:8-9; 1 Cor. 12:18-20, 25); diverse gifts working together; weaker are essential; mutual concern (Rom. 12:22-26)	Ministry builds upon the efforts of the different parts, regardless of the role; harmony so all the members care for each other
Sharing truth in love, healthy growth (Eph. 4:15-16); sharpening each other's character (Prov. 27:17)	Transparency with each other; truth shared for healthier and fruitful mutuality; constructive feedback; differences result in something better
United in mind, love, spirit and purpose (Phil. 2:2-5)	Unity even though the composition is diverse
Example of Euodia and Syntyche (Phil. 4:2-3)	Knowing people by name

Table 1: Polycentric Mission

---

[14] Sam George, "Motus Dei (the Move of God)," in *Global Migration & Christian Faith: Implications for Identity and Mission*, ed. M. Daniel Carroll R. and Vincent E. Bacote (Eugene: Cascade Books, 2021), 178.

[15] George, "Motus Dei (the Move of God)," in *Global Migration & Christian Faith: Implications for Identity and Mission*, 178.

(3) Holistic: Donald Senior calls one portrayal of mission in the New Testament the 'community of healing and reconciliation'.[16] Jay Matenga characterises the 'Good News preached throughout the whole world [as] a promise, not a task to be fulfilled'.[17] Western mission made it a task to be achieved. This shifts the 'focus to an unhealthy and unbiblical anthropocentric perspective of the mission of God.'[18] The kingdom of God in the context of the global church is 'a missional framework [that is] broader than the salvation narrative of God's redemption and forgiveness [that] subsumes the issue of forgiveness and eternal life within the larger context of entering the Kingdom'.[19] The Majority World's 'epistemology [study of knowledge] includes the miraculous, the supernatural, signs, wonders, dreams, intuitions and feelings as an integral part of how people perceive truth'.[20]

Mission focuses on the reconciliation, renewal, and restoration of the kingdom of God, of which the worship community of Christ is the sign and foretaste. Relationship and companionship drive ministry and co-creation. Rupen Das notes how 'God's mission… of redeeming, reconciling and restoring all creation… is greater than anything that Christians and the church can envisage, and [God] invites his people to partner with him in it.'[21]

(4) Self-theologising: There is a need to update the three-self theory of church development introduced by Rufus Anderson and Henry Venn in the nineteenth century. They believed that younger churches (on the mission field) would more readily become independent through principles of self-supporting, self-governing, and self-propagating. Through the rise of the global church paradigm, greater expectations are placed on Mission Theology, missional hermeneutics, praxis, and faithful witness to become polycentric, polyphonic, and polymodal, reflecting self-theologising local theologies. Sung Chan Kwon sees how up until now ministry has 'been standardized by outsiders'.[22] The development of local missional theologies, leadership models, training strategies, and a deeper understanding of God at work all become of greater importance. This is needed to assist the Majority World church, which may face challenges of reconciling its Christian mission history as it establishes its indigenous identity instead of representing a Western religion. It also faces sociopolitical issues including corruption, authoritarian governments, oppression, persecution, minority status, interfaith relations, conflict, peace-building, cultural values, and rituals.

In response, some call for a fourth self to add to the three-self mission theory. For example, Das adds 'selfhood' to counter 'a lack of "self-initiative" in the Majority World church'.[23] This creates opportunities 'to develop local missional

---

[16] Donald Senior, "Correlating Images of Church and Images of Mission in the New Testament," *Missiology: An International Review* 13, no. 1 (1995): 7.

[17] Matenga, 8.

[18] Matenga, 8.

[19] Das, 204.

[20] Das, 204.

[21] Das, 207.

[22] Das, 212.

[23] Das, 204.

theologies and strategies, understand local models of leadership and training… and gain a greater awareness of how God is already working in the Global South'.[24] Patrick Fung calls for 'an international hermeneutical community, partnering together, in which leaders from different parts of the global church help one another to understand the Bible from various cultural contexts and check one another's cultural biases'.[25] Kwon states that now, 'local leaders… root themselves in the Word of God' instead of simply accepting 'the interpretation of others' and they learn how to 'participate in the mission of God with their own gifts and strengths'.[26]

(5) Giving agency: Majority World mission may still have 'an identity challenge that is decolonized from the era from which these organizations started'.[27] This can be expressed as feelings of inferiority. This calls for new approaches for listening 'to what Majority World voices are saying about the future of missions'.[28] Those outside the Majority World need to learn how 'not to dominate' but instead what it means to be 'sent to dwell'.[29]

Agency is the 'capability to exert influence over one's functioning and the course of events by one's actions'.[30] Agency is needed for Majority World missions within global relationships because agency means 'the freedom to make unrestricted and independent choices'.[31] Majority World missions require agency 'to determine their own futures and forge their own identities [and]… contribute meaningfully'.[32] Discernment by Majority World missions may be needed to figure out how to effectively use their agency within 'the much larger and more powerful international partners' structure [and] to work out their decision-making status within the larger mission structure'.[33]

Gaps Between the Paradigms

Gaps between the two paradigms are to be expected. The Christendom paradigm is still influencing our understanding and practice of mission and will only be replaced by the new through long and highly complex processes. In recent years

[24] Das, 212.

[25] Patrick Fung, "Mission Partnership in a Polycentric World," in *Majority World Perspectives on Christian Mission*, ed. Eugene Baron and Nico Botha (Auckland Park: University of Johannesburg Press, 2022), 56.

[26] Sung Chan Kwon, *A Missional Reading of the Fourth Gospel: A Gospel-Driven Theology of Discipleship* (Oxford: Regnum, 2022), 6.

[27] Kirk Franklin, "Implications of Identity in Global Mission," *Missiology: An International Review* 51, no. 1 (2023): 9, https://dx.doi.org/10.1177/00918296221117709.

[28] Das, 199.

[29] Matenga, 8.

[30] Albert Bandura, "Toward an Agentic Theory of the Self," *Advances in Self Research* 3 (2008): 16.

[31] Graham Hill, and Grace Ji-Sun Kim, *Healing Our Broken Humanity* (Downers Grove: IVP, 2018), 128.

[32] Hill, and Kim, 128.

[33] Franklin, "Implications of Identity in Global Mission," 5.

there has been an almost frantic obsession to anticipate and recognise the next paradigm in mission. If the paradigm is shifting, what is it shifting towards? Do we really want to see something new or simply make the Christendom mission model work better?

The step Matenga suggests is to identify 'the gaps in the Industrial (e.g. Christendom paradigm) melody' and amplify 'the Indigenous (e.g. global church paradigm) voice so their melody can be heard'. This 'is true of culturally diverse missions groups' and in particular 'between expatriate and national believers'.[34] In addition, Matenga observes how God has provided the church with 'people called to transboundary service' who transcend the gulf between the Industrial and Indigenous epistemes.[35] This calls for 'a unity that celebrates diversity and requires holding or sitting [with] the tensions of difference [between the two paradigms], allowing them to transform us. Because… you cannot create harmony without tension.'[36] The opportunity is provided to 'counterpoint' the two paradigms (or what Matenga calls 'epistemes') and 'hold them in tension and tune the difference to create a wonderful, if uncomfortable and sometimes painful, shalom harmony' that exposes 'gaps in the Industrial ecosystem of knowing' in order to 'then amplify some strengths in the values of the Indigenous realm'.[37]

The shift between the two paradigms can create pain, tension, and distortions. We now explore the issues of (1) power imbalance and (2) reductionism.

(1) Power imbalance: Western nations use their neo-colonialism and its domination of resources, influence, and associated cultural power over other parts of the world, which affects global mission. According to Das, the Christendom paradigm does 'not acknowledge or appreciate the growing contribution of indigenous missions in the Majority World unless they were funded or resourced by Western churches'.[38] Das also recognises how 'Majority World mission leaders feel wounded by the treatment they receive from Western evangelicals and mission leaders. They often feel talked down to and not trusted. Their opinions are not valued.'[39] However, Matenga states, 'we are in no position any longer to approach missions with a superior and impositional attitude' but instead, 'we now must go into all the world with a humble and genuinely servant-learner attitude'.[40]

Another observable power imbalance occurs when Western resources ensure the continued domination of Western theologising and praxis. For example, Das notes: 'Western worldviews, theological frameworks, strategies, and funding still dominate most discussions and literature on mission, evangelism, and theological education.'[41]

---

[34] Matenga, 7.

[35] Matenga, 8.

[36] Matenga, 6.

[37] Matenga, 3.

[38] Das, 210.

[39] Das, 210.

[40] Matenga, 7.

[41] Das, 198.

Power imbalance takes the form of colonial affiliations; unhelpful use of power, money, and other resources; and attitudes of cultural, educational, spiritual, and material superiority.

(2) Reductionism: Managerial mission displays a form of reductionism through its requirements of the Christendom paradigm on the global church, and according to Das, reveals how 'the management systems required for funding proposals, reporting, evaluations, rigid implementation schedules, and personnel management were too onerous and of questionable value'.[42] Samuel Escobar notes how managerial mission came from organisations with church growth and the AD2000 and Beyond movement. It was 'an effort to reduce Christian mission to a manageable enterprise'.[43] Missional action was streamlined into a linear sequence of logical steps to solve a problem through objective-oriented management. However, Majority World mission and even Western mission leaders wonder how 'is this information ever used?'[44]

The efforts of Christian mission spread to every part of the world, and churches were established. At that time, with little questioning or examination, and therefore with a reductionist mindset, new mission movements from the Majority World brought an understanding and practice of mission shaped by the Christendom paradigm reflected in European migration, colonialism, and a call to civilise the world.

Another form of reductionism in the Christendom mission paradigm is its focus on sending, which may lead to ignoring how the church now exists in every nation, in close proximity to those still without visible witness in their own communities. This 'local' church has access to all peoples, nations, tribes, and languages. Furthermore, the focus on the 'sent one' risks obscuring how church growth has happened in the global church paradigm when local Christians have taken the initiative to reach out and live out their faith.

Friendship as the Language of Mission

Now that we have mentioned the gaps and the problem of power imbalances and reductionism in mission relationships, we need insights into how to bridge these gaps. The answer lies in building friendships and learning to listen.

To set this part of mission history in context, over 100 years ago, the 1910 World Missionary Conference in Edinburgh gathered church and mission leaders from around the world, though mainly from the Western world, where most of those involved in mission came from at the time. During the conference in Edinburgh, the theme of friendship, which furthered our understanding of mission, was presented powerfully and unforgettably to the global mission community's attention through a remarkable and enduring intervention.

---

[42] Das, 210.

[43] Samuel Escobar, "Managerial Missiology," in *Dictionary of World Mission*, ed. John Corrie (Downers Grove: IVP Academic, 2007), 216.

[44] Das, 210.

A young Anglican minister from India named Samuel Azariah (1874–1945) was invited to participate in the conference, one of only 17 representatives from the Majority World.[45] Asked to address the participants, he spoke about the Indian Christian community's appreciation for Western foreign missionaries' work, self-giving, and sacrifice. Then he boldly addressed 'the condescending attitude of Western missionaries toward non-Western Christians'.[46] He concluded,

> Through the ages to come the Indian Church will rise up in gratitude to attest the heroism and self-denying labours of the missionary body. You have given your goods to feed the poor. You have given your bodies to be burned. We also ask for *love*. Give us FRIENDS![47]

This call by Azariah is remembered as one of the most noteworthy statements from the conference. To grow as a global church in mission requires us to address this fundamental issue of friendship. Yet, a century later, according to Dana Robert, the church is still burdened with 'friendships strained by postcolonialism, dependency, paternalism and poverty'.[48] Azariah had noted how the majority of Western missionaries who had come to serve in India failed to get 'rid of an air of patronage and [arrogance] in establishing a genuinely brotherly and happy relation as between equals with their Indian flocks'.[49] While he commended these missionaries for their good works, he recognised that most Western missionaries had failed in the significant area of creating friendships in their partnering relationships with the Indians.

What does it mean to be true friends in the mission of God? Our loving God functions as a triune friendship community, and he invites us into that relationship. Friendship is a basic and essential quality we offer to each other: those without Christ, and those whom God is inviting into his kingdom.

Closely related to friendship, the theme of partnership was addressed at the 1947 World Missionary Conference held in Whitby, Canada. World War II had ended in 1945, and the world was healing from deep divisions. The 112 participants who came focused on evaluating how mission efforts were affected by the war. They humbly recognised the necessity for a new awareness of partnership in mission across the global church. Discussions explored how the 'witness of the church' needed to take place as a 'partnership in obedience [in other words] as the obedient partnering between all Christian churches and initiatives'.[50] Our understanding of partnership grows as the church engages in new and different frontiers. Whether these frontiers are cross-cultural or not, the church must engage them in partnership. We need partnerships involving those

---

[45] David Kerr, and Kenneth Ross, "Introduction," in *Edinburgh 2010: Mission Then and Now*, ed. David Kerr and Kenneth Ross (Oxford: Regnum, 2009), 3.

[46] Yeh, 110.

[47] Brian Stanley, *The World Missionary Conference, Edinburgh 1910* (Grand Rapids: Wm B. Eerdmans, 2009), 125.

[48] Balia, and Kim, 133.

[49] Dana Robert, "Cross-Cultural Friendship in the Creation of Twentieth-Century World Christianity," *International Bulletin of Missionary Research* 35, no. 2 (2011): 100.

[50] Wrogemann, 64.

from outside and those already together in local and global communities. We need partnerships between diaspora Christians and indigenous Christians. We need partnerships between congregations and specialist groups in mission. We even need authentic partnerships between Christians and those of other faiths; those with a shared commitment to righteousness and justice. We, as evangelicals, do not need to be afraid of these kinds of partnerships but to trust that God will work through them for his glory as we keep the Lordship of Christ central in what we do.

Through these two historical encounters in 1910 and 1947, we see the topic of partnering in mission gaining attention. Learning from the past calls for awareness of history when we approach issues of importance in mission. Or as expressed in Ecclesiastes: 'History merely repeats itself. It has all been done before. Nothing under the sun is truly new' (1:9, NLT).

When Azariah made the call for friendship as part of the partnering approaches of Western missionaries in his country of India, he was committed to cross-cultural friendship because he observed its power. He pleaded his case for a visible demonstration of the Christian vision of God's kingdom to his fractured Indian society. His country needed to witness the church bound 'together across the dividing lines of caste, ethnicity, culture and empire' by a unique quality of friendship that 'derived from the knowledge… of the exceeding riches of the glory of Christ'.[51]

Friendship with God, each other, and those we are called to serve is a foundational missiological principle for the post-Christendom mission, giving God glory and presenting a visible demonstration of his kingdom. Friendship takes place within and also creates and deepens community. Participants in the community of mission share common characteristics and commitments. God's mission would be served more profoundly if every partnership and collaborative effort in global church mission had the foundation of generous friendship.

Let us consider how friendship in mission can be deepened.

Listening: The global church in mission needs to listen to the voices representing the church and 'harmonise' with each other as friends in God's mission. However, it is extraordinarily challenging in our world today to genuinely listen. Pervasive noise from places of power, even within the bounds of mission, is increasing and becoming more diverse. The result can interfere with hearing and discerning the essential from the non-essential. Learning to listen to those different from us is paramount if we're truly serious about engaging in God's mission. We need to develop a posture of respect, curiosity, and openness to others and struggle to overcome being shaped by our assumptions and unconscious biases, which stem from our experiences, gender, age, and contexts. Those unconscious biases make it almost impossible to hear what is different. Research has shown that we do not hear and see what we cannot comprehend. Yet, God leads through his Spirit. He speaks through people regardless of their role, status, or culture. Consequently, the global church

---

[51] Stanley, 129–30.

community in mission experiences the beauty of diversity within the body of Christ and demonstrates how each part blends within the symphony of voices.

God's global body consists 'of many voices or sounds',[52] a definition of polyphonism. There are many voices represented by the multiethnic body of Christ. However, the history of the modern missionary era was set to a Western Christendom paradigm tonal system. That's not what the polyphonic global body of Christ sounds like today. The biblical insights, concepts, and benefits of polyphonic mission can be seen here, in Table 2.

Polyphonic (many voices)	
Biblical insights	**Concepts and Benefits**
Speech that heals (Prov. 15:4)	Attentive space of learning, listening, voicing
Speech and teaching of good/wise person (Prov. 10:21); wise speech (Prov. 15:2); speech that spreads knowledge (Prov. 15:7)	Diverse voices, insights, discernment, building real relationships; mutual learning
Benefits of many advisers (Prov. 15:22); listening brings discernment and understanding (Prov. 15:22)	Wisdom and discernment come through the counsel and voices of many
Quick to listen (Jas. 1:19)	Careful and thoughtful listening to each other
Sounds must be clear to be understood (1 Cor. 14:7); clarity brings correct response (1 Cor. 14:7)	Harmonious, beauty of diverse voices; listening with integrity and respect

Table 2: Polyphonic Mission

Third Spaces: If we are striving for partnership, genuinely listening to each other, and are willing to step out from the limits of our own worlds, then creating a Third Space can be very beneficial. Third Space theory involves participants leaving their own safe spaces and stepping into a third space where they can own their assumptions, beliefs, and perspectives while remaining open to hearing others and, together, creating something new. Establishing these safe spaces enables different groups to come together to acknowledge, explore, discuss, understand, celebrate, reconcile, and develop new friendships, ideas, and concepts in and for God's mission. Each part of the body is necessary, and our role is to ensure that the body is healthy, growing, and effective. Rather than addressing a conflict or decision in a binary sense – a 'right' way or a 'wrong' way – negotiating a third way is often preferable. The third way may be a new option or it may be a creative blending of ideas from numerous voices. This promotes interdependent cooperation of giving, receiving, and serving one another, demonstrating respect and dignity in authentic partnerships based on genuine friendships in mission.

Stewardship and generosity: In true generosity, the value of each participant is recognised and affirmed. Sometimes it's harder to receive than to give; some

---

[52] "Polyphonic," accessed 20 May 2020, ttps://www.dictionary.com/browse/polyphonic.

parts of the body need to learn how to receive, and others how to give. Good stewardship becomes the habitual behaviour of friends serving together within God's mission. The 'strengthening of friendship [in mission leads] to greater collaboration, partnership, and generosity… Stewardship and generosity encompass all of life and include time, service, compassion, grace, and our whole being, not only our finances. Stewardship and generosity envision all of God's Church as both givers and receivers.'[53]

Generosity is central to mission of the global church and warrants more extensive exploration. Scott Rodin states, 'Generous stewards in God's kingdom reveal selfless service to one's neighbour and to creation. Such stewards are generous in response to God's "immeasurable generosity" in Jesus Christ.'[54] Generosity is about 'readiness or liberality in giving'[55]; being kind and generous to offer more of something – especially money – than is strictly necessary or expected. 'Christ-centred generosity is the disposition [or character] of a heart that is rich toward God and is a defining characteristic of the life of an obedient and joyful steward.'[56]

The Old Testament gives many examples of generosity. For example:

- '… be openhanded and freely lend them whatever they need' (Deut. 15:8, NIV).
- '… bring a gift in proportion to the way the LORD your God has blessed you' (Deut. 16:17, NIV).
- 'A generous person will prosper; whoever refreshes others will be refreshed' (Prov. 11:25, NIV).
- 'Whoever is kind to the poor lends to the LORD, and he will reward them for what they have done' (Prov. 19:17, NIV).

In the New Testament generosity is expressed in many ways. For example:

- 'Give, and you will receive. Your gift will return to you in full – pressed down, shaken together to make room for more, running over, and poured into your lap. The amount you give will determine the amount you get back' (Luke 6:38, NLT).
- 'In his grace, God has given us different gifts for doing certain things well… And if you have a gift for showing kindness to others, do it gladly' (Rom. 12:6-8, NLT).
- 'They [the churches in Macedonia] are being tested by many troubles, and they are very poor. But they are also filled with abundant joy, which has

---

[53] Susan Van Wynen, Dave Crough, and Kirk Franklin, "Foundational Statements of the Wycliffe Global Alliance," 2019, accessed 7 September, 2020, https://www.wycliffe.net/wp-content/uploads/2020/01/Alliance_Foundational_Statements_2019_09_EN.pdf.

[54] Kirk Franklin, and Nelus Niemandt, "Funding God's Mission: Towards a Missiology of Generosity," *Missionalia* 43, no. 3 (2015): 389.

[55] Generosity," accessed 30 September 2021, https://www.dictionary.com/browse/generosity.

[56] R. Scott Rodin, "A Vision for the Generous Life," in *Christ-Centered Generosity: Global Perspectives on the Biblical Call to a Generous Life*, ed. R. Scott Rodin (Colbert: Kingdom Life Publishers, 2015), 11.

overflowed in rich generosity. For I can testify that they gave not only what they could afford, but far more. And they did it of their own free will' (2 Cor. 8:2-3, NLT).

Biblical insight urges members of the body of Christ to be united, to work together in agreement, to grow, be fruitful, and sharpen one another as like-minded companions, bearing one another's burdens, and accomplishing more together. We are to be gracious, a blessing, be openhanded, lend, share wealth, give gifts of grace out of our abundance, and be generous. All of these contribute to our biblical foundation of partnering and collaboration as friends and stewards of God's mission in the global church.

More practical examples include:

• intercession and spiritual warfare to break through spiritual barriers;

• solidarity in suffering, through our presence and friendship, even in the most difficult of circumstances – a powerful witness to our oneness in Christ, making not only an impact around us but in the heavenly realm (Eph. 3:10). This solidarity includes advocacy, coordinating practical support, and prayer.

The Language of Faithful Witness

As we explore the concerns around the language of mission, especially as influenced by the Christendom paradigm, 'faithful witness' is an alternative way of thinking and talking about mission.[57] Faithful witness can be pictured through these overlapping spheres represented in Diagram 1.

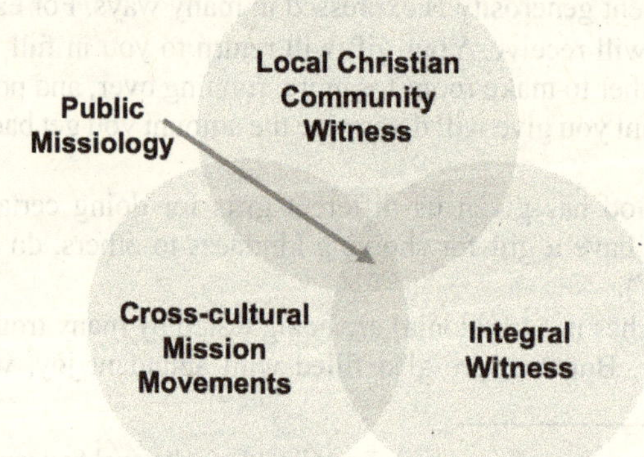

Diagram 1: The Spheres of Faithful Witness

Local Christian community witness: The body of Christ in a local context gathered in worship and witness as well as visible through members of the Body

---

[57] The sections 'Local Christian community witness', 'Cross-cultural mission movements', and 'Integral witness' have been adapted from the author's work with OCMS's Research Forum for Faithful Witness (https://www.ocms.ac.uk/research-forum/).

involved in their communities in faithful witness. These individuals and groups may be in local churches, regional groups of churches, or other groupings of Jesus followers. Witness can be found in every aspect of society. There are places where witness breaks down between different parts of the body of Christ and this needs to be acknowledged and addressed.

Cross-cultural mission movements: Individuals and teams moving from their own ethno-linguistic communities and cultures into other cultural spaces in faithful witness. In the process, cross-cultural witness takes shape. Historically, this has involved specialists (missionaries) and often included moving to another place, with the goal of establishing churches. Creating intercultural relationships has become a means of witness and takes place within every context.

Integral witness: Individuals and groups of Christians whose focus is on the kingdom of God, seeking to bring the Lordship of Christ into every sphere of life. Historically, the integral mission movement has been located in Non-Governmental Organisations (NGOs) and Faith-based Organisations (FBOs) and has tended to focus on societal transformation. It now includes integral witness through business and the marketplace. It calls upon the need to resource and equip those who work in the profit marketplace and secular social enterprise for integral witness.

Public missiology: Each of our circles includes the question of public missiology, which is defined as 'congregational witness that moves back and forth across all "spaces" of public life in order to weave a thickness of persons of the Trinity for the flourishing of all of life'.[58]

When the language of faithful witness is inclusive, it helps us conceptualise and develop mission for the coming century. Faithful witness has the potential to bring together into mission the three critical strands of cross-cultural mission movements, local Christian community witness, and the integration of the whole of life. When we consider conventional cross-cultural mission, we may still be operating from and using the language of 'heroes' or 'pioneers' in our mobilisation efforts. When we reframe our understanding of what the roles are for participants in cross-cultural faithful witness, we need to incorporate the participation of all parts of the church in the reign of God and what that entails.

Summary

We established how paradigms and their shifts help us interpret the church's history in mission. When applied to Mission Theology, they provide a framework to analyse and interpret the changing context of the global church and how this emerging paradigm is underway, shifting from Christendom to post-Christianity and the growth of the global church in the lands of the Majority World. This has been a multifaceted, polycentric, and polyphonic movement.

Whether through friendship, partnership, generosity, or anything else, we need to develop our Mission Theology mindfully and methodically. As we do, we will be better positioned to improve and strengthen our service in God's

---

[58] Okesson, 95–96.

mission. That is our invitation: to focus on developing Mission Theology in all its richness so our contributions achieve an enduring difference in the areas or spheres where God invites our contribution.

Reflective Questions:

- As you consider mission moving into the twenty-first century and the era of the global church, what significant issues are already affecting the effectiveness of mission?
- Are these issues, in your opinion, receiving enough attention within the global church? If not, do any fall within your areas of interest and reflection? If so, how could you incorporate them in further exploration?

PART TWO

MISSION THEOLOGY

5. Building Blocks of Mission Theology

Introduction

In this chapter, we explore the goal of Mission Theology, which is to help us understand and participate more effectively in God's mission in all its fullness, applying his mission to the infinite characteristics of human society and the world God has called us to steward. Mission Theology is interested in the assumptions and underlying principles which determine the Christian faith in terms of the motivation, message, methods, strategies, and goals of Christian mission.

Our mission derives from God's mission and contains concepts far more profound than the sending aspect, centred on the reign of God expressed through the Lordship of Christ. Summarised by the Apostle Paul, the mystery of God's purposes, hidden for generations, is now fully revealed in Christ. What are those purposes? In the fullness of time, God will 'bring everything together under the authority of Christ – everything in heaven and on earth' (Eph. 1:10, NLT). This fullness, *pléróma* (Greek), refers to what has come to completeness in Christ. As René Padilla observed, mission describes everyone, and everything brought together under the Lordship of Christ.[1]

God's Mission (*Missio Dei*)

God is both engaged in and the source of mission. In theological terms, this is referred to as the *missio Dei*, Latin for the mission of God. *Missio Dei* is the salvation activity of the triune missionary God, flowing from his nature through the loving, sacrificial service of his Son. God extends the gift of salvation to all people, inviting them through new life in Christ into the community of his kingdom.

God's mission belongs to him, not the church or individuals. Mark Simon notes how the *missio Dei* 'draws attention to the principle that God rather than the church is the initiator and source of mission, and that mission is an attribute of the triune God, particularly his sending love. The *missio Dei* has as its goal "the establishment of the lordship of Christ over the entire redeemed creation."'[2]

---

[1] René Padilla, "The Mission of the Church in Light of the Kingdom of God," *Transformation* 1, no. 2 (1984).
[2] Mark A. Simon, *Living to the Praise of God's Glory: A Missional Reading of Ephesians* (Eugene: Wipf & Stock, 2021), 39.

Mission Theology (Missiology)

Mission Theology, or missiology, as some prefer to call it, is 'a branch of theology',[3] the academic study of mission, sometimes referred to as 'mission studies'.[4] It is the 'science of missions',[5] 'a systematic and scientific study'[6] to 'investigate scientifically'[7] all activities associated with 'the fulfilment of God's mission',[8] 'the missionary dimension of the Christian faith, the Great Commission'.[9] Missiology explores 'the fact that the church is missionary by nature' and examines 'critically the activities through which the church does her mission'.[10] Missiology, therefore, is:

- an academic discipline;
- part of theology;
- a science that uses systematised knowledge and investigation;
- focused on the mission of God and the church in mission.

Interdisciplinary Nature

The study of the mission of God, what we're calling Mission Theology, is integrated within theology and mission and, therefore, not peripheral to the study of theology. Mission Theology 'concerns the God of mission and the mission of God. This means that all theological categories are inherently missiological and all missionary activities are profoundly theological'.[11]

Charles Van Engen states that Mission Theology's 'object of study and reflection is the entire field of missiology which itself is multi- and interdisciplinary'.[12] It is interdependent with theology, biblical studies, history, and social sciences. Together, these inform mission praxis and the interface of reflection and action. While Mission Theology is interdisciplinary, it 'is a unified whole [and] is a discipline in its own right, centred on Jesus Christ and his mission'.[13] Mission Theology helps us to gauge our proximity to or distance from

---

[3] Oborji, 42.

[4] Oborji, 42.

[5] John Mark Terry, Ebbie Smith, and Justice Anderson, *Missiology: An Introduction to the Foundations, History, and Strategies of World Missions* (Nashville: Broadman & Holman Publishers, 1998), 8.

[6] Oborji, 42.

[7] Johannes Verkuyl, *Contemporary Missiology: An Introduction* (Grand Rapids: Wm B. Eerdmans, 1978), 5.

[8] Kenneth Nehrbass, *Advance Missiology: How to Study Missions in Credible and Useful Ways* (Eugene: Cascade Books, 2021), 14.

[9] Francis Anekwe Oborji, *Towards African Missiology: Issues of New Language for African Christianity*, vol. 1 (Bloomington: Xlibris, 2020), 3.

[10] Oborji, *Concepts of Mission: The Evolution of Contemporary Missiology*, 42.

[11] John Corrie, "Introduction," in *Dictionary of Mission Theology: Evangelical Foundations*, ed. John Corrie (Downers Grove: IVP Academic, 2007), xv.

[12] Charles Van Engen, *Transforming Mission Theology* (Pasadena: William Carey Library, 2017), 21.

[13] Van Engen, 21.

the centre, Jesus Christ, and in doing so, we evaluate whether the diverse disciplines under review take us beyond a point of being relevant to the centre.

Parameters

As we consider Mission Theology and its boundaries, drawing on the ideas of bounded and centred sets may be helpful. A bounded set is defined by the edges or borders that exclude what it is not. For example, nationality is a bounded set. You are either 'in' or 'out', a citizen and part of the bounded set of that nationality, or you are outside of that; you are different.

The concept of a bounded set confining Mission Theology within lines of certain assumptions and propositions is counterproductive, even detrimental. Instead, we view Mission Theology as a centred set, where the centre holds great significance. What belongs or doesn't belong to a centred set is not defined by a boundary but rather by the relation to the centre and movement towards or away from the centre. In this case, consider Jesus Christ and his Lordship at the centre, with Mission Theology assisting us in reflecting on that centre and encompassing everything that enables us to move towards this centre.

However, when we look back through history and even today through the lens of a bounded set, only some have placed Jesus Christ at the centre of their understanding and practice of mission. For example, the seventeenth-century Dutch theologian Gisbertus Voetius understood the centre of Mission Theology as the conversion of the heathen, planting of churches, and the glory of God. For William Carey, who has had such an impact on the modern mission movement in so many ways, the Great Commission in Matthew 28:18-20 defined for him what was at the centre of mission. Pietism put the lostness of humanity at the centre. Vatican II put the people of God at the centre. In 1968, the WCC placed humanisation and the pain of God, the cross, bearing witness in six continents, ecumenical unity, the covenant, and liberation at the centre. Donald McGavran put the discipling of all *ethne* at the centre. David Bosch placed the God of history, compassion, and transformation at the centre. The kingdom of God was at the centre for Arthur Glasser.[14] For John Stott, the centre was all God sends us into the world to be and do.

Mission Theology helps us bring together who we are, what we know, and what we do in mission. Through Mission Theology, we integrate our faith in Jesus Christ, God's presence, the church's theological reflection through the centuries, constant new reading of Scripture, the hermeneutics of our contexts, our journey in discipleship, and our understanding of our ultimate purpose and meaning of the church in God's mission.

Mission Theology assists our movement between the centre and outer limits of the multiple academic disciplines that help us understand mission theory and practice. It constantly leads us towards integration, deeper insight, and mutual enrichment in those disciplines. Further, it questions, clarifies, integrates, and expands the assumptions of those various related disciplines.

---

[14] Van Engen, 22.

Considering Mission Theology as a centred set, its centre is vital and often contested. Discovering your framework and centre of Mission Theology and what draws it together will guide how you work with and benefit from it.

Studying Mission Theology

Ross Langmead observes that Mission Theology is 'a separate focus of study [and] a relative newcomer in theological education. In many theological circles, it is still marginal.'[15] Mission Theology has always been multidisciplinary, bringing together various domains or disciplines from which the students and researchers of mission draw understanding. It was the nineteenth-century German theologian Martin Kähler who said that 'mission is the mother of theology',[16] or in other words, 'theology… was an accompanying manifestation of Christian mission'.[17] As the church engages and participates in God's mission, it is compelled to recognise who God is and God at work, and consequently to form a theological understanding. Whether recognised or not, mission lies at the heart of the theological process, and when it doesn't, theology becomes rather abstract and even unhelpful.

Mission Theology holds an important and interdependent role within the framework of theology. Langmead observes that as the global church develops its '… sense of mission there is a need for missiology – both as a dimension of all theological studies and also as a subject area – to assist in providing a strong missional direction to the whole enterprise of theology and theological education'.[18]

Mission Theory and Practice

Mission Theology is interdisciplinary, drawing on numerous disciplines such as theology, biblical studies, history, social sciences, and contributions from mission praxis. Praxis, conversely, describes the interface between theory and action – the processes by which theories become embedded and lived out in practice. Mission praxis, therefore, is a significant part of forming Mission Theology. This is shown in Diagram 2.

---

[15] Ross Langmead, "What Is Missiology?," *Missiology: An International Review* 42, no. 1 (2013): 67.

[16] Martin Kähler, 1971, quoted in Bosch, *Transforming Mission: Paradigm Shifts in Theology of Mission*, 16.

[17] Oborji, *Towards African Missiology: Issues of New Language for African Christianity*, xiv.

[18] Langmead, 67.

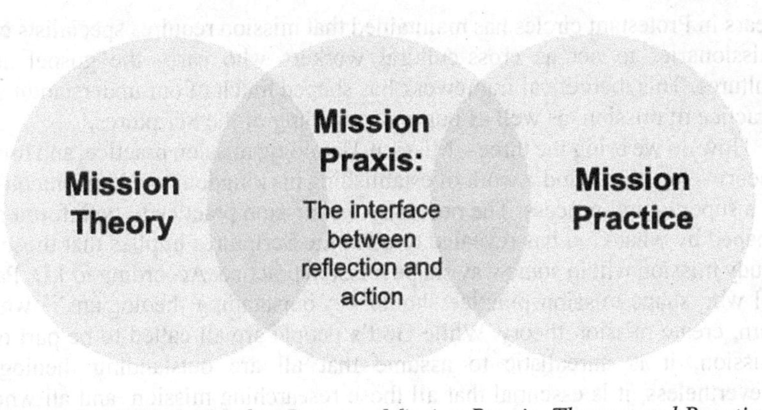

Mission Theory | **Mission Praxis:** The interface between reflection and action | **Mission Practice**

Diagram 2: The Relationship Between Mission Praxis, Theory, and Practice

Timothy Tennent expresses concern that 'missiology as a modern discipline has been dominated by the social sciences', while acknowledging valuable insights from anthropology and sociology to missiology.[19] The Bible uses non-biblical sources. For example, history in Numbers 21:14-15 ('This is why it is said Book of the Wars of the Lord…', NET); poetry in Acts 17:28 ('as even some of your own poets have said, "For we too are his offspring"' – '… from Aratus (ca. 310–245 BC)', NET); and eye-witness sources in Luke 1:1-2 ('Now many have undertaken to compile an account of the things that have been fulfilled among us, like the accounts passed on to us by those who were eyewitnesses and servants of the word from the beginning', NET). These examples help us appreciate why social sciences are helpful. However, placing too much emphasis on these fields creates an 'anthropocentric and shallow' foundation because 'Christianity as a whole, is built on an entirely different foundation and worldview'.[20] This means 'the controlling categories' of mission should be 'theological, not sociological'.[21]

Mission theory has not always kept pace systematically with mission praxis. To address this issue, consider the following areas where the principles and methods that form mission theory developed from praxis:

- Mission theory requires a theoretical framework that provides an effective scholarly foundation for missional studies.
- This theory should have the full extent of mission in view – historical, sociological, and contextual factors, theological issues, and expectations of mission practice.
- Mission theory should provide an authoritative voice for mission studies that will guide other disciplines related to missiology.

In practice, Mission Theology, mission praxis, and mission theory each progress at different rates. For example, mission theory for much of the last 200+

---

¹⁹ Tennent, 60.
²⁰ Tennent, 60.
²¹ Tennent, 60.

years in Protestant circles has maintained that mission requires specialists called missionaries to act as cross-cultural workers who carry the gospel across cultures. This theoretical framework has shaped much of our understanding and practice of mission, as well as our understanding of the Scriptures.

How do we bring the three – Mission Theology, mission practice, and mission theory – together? God's work of establishing his kingdom and his righteousness is a supernatural process. The necessity for mission practice to be informed and shaped by what God has revealed to us in the Scriptures implies that those who study mission will in some way shape mission practice. According to J.D. Payne, all who shape mission practice should be 'outstanding theologians'[22] who, in turn, create mission theory. While God's people are all called to be part of his mission, it is unrealistic to assume that all are outstanding theologians. Nevertheless, it is essential that all those researching mission, and all who are involved in shaping mission practice, can integrate mission theological reflection into their work. All areas that call for further research to inform mission cry out for the Lordship of Christ to be understood and owned. Consequently, studying Mission Theology represents the starting point of this journey. This is shown in Diagram 3.

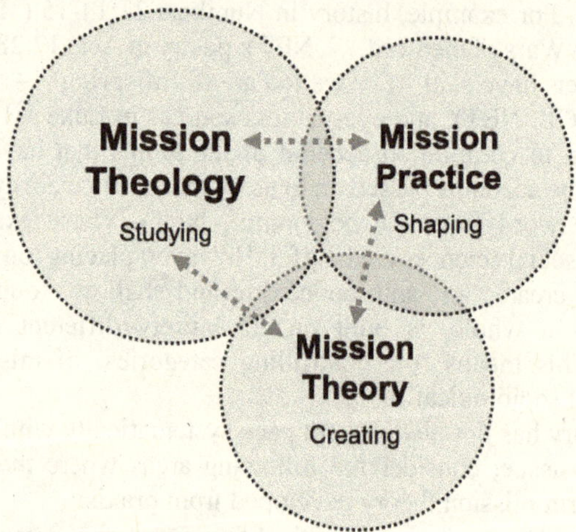

Diagram 3: Relationship Between Mission Theology, Practice, and Theory

The missiologist and mission theorist must be concerned that mission theory contributes to realities faced in mission practice. If mission practice is to be taken seriously in today's global mission context, practitioners should consider a framework or frameworks for understanding and studying Mission Theology, as well as the need to identify the key topics of importance for missiological study and reflection.

---

[22] J.D. Payne, "Introduction," in *Missionary Methods: Research, Reflections and Realities*, ed. Craig Ott and J.D. Payne (Pasadena: William Carey Library, 2013), xvi.

Frameworks for Mission Theology

How do we develop a framework to unite these components, integrating Mission Theology into our praxis? Here are some examples of models for mission theory.

In his 1987 textbook *Introduction to Missiology*, Allan Tippett suggested that missiology held a position between two other fields, and the linkages were not often obvious:
1. theology, theory, and history of mission and anthropology (social, theory, and history of mission);
2. anthropology (social, theoretical, and applied).[23]

Since then, further refinement has taken place. For example, David Hesselgrave describes three types of source materials required for a foundation that enables and informs missional inquiry, research, and reflection:
1. the Bible, church beliefs or creeds, and related theological methodology;
2. the social and behavioural sciences;
3. mission biography and history.[24]

Michael Pocock points out the need for three integrated systems that bring understanding to missiological questions and concerns:
1. theology;
2. missionary experience;
3. the systems and contributions from various fields of social sciences, including 'anthropology, sociology, psychology, communications, linguistics, demography, geography, and statistics'.[25]

Craig Ott identifies three interdisciplinary subjects needed for the study of missional methods:
1. theology;
2. mission history;
3. social science.[26]

J.D. Payne provides a foundation for missiological reflection, which informs missional methods and practice. According to Payne, missional methods should be established through a reflective process that begins with and regularly returns to the Bible and missiological study of one's context. He presents three foundations for the study of missional theory, positioning them in order:
1. theology and biblical studies as the base level;
2. missiology as the middle level;
3. missionary methods as the top level.[27]

In summary, according to the missiologists surveyed, missiological studies

---

[23] Alan Tippett, *Introduction to Missiology* (Pasadena: William Carey Library, 1987), xii.

[24] David Hesselgrave, "Preface," in *Missiology and the Social Sciences: Contributions, Cautions and Conclusions*, ed. Rommen Ed and Gary Corwin (Pasadena: William Carey Library, 1996), 1.

[25] Michael Pocock, "Introduction: An Appeal for Balance," in *Missiology and the Social Sciences: Contributions, Cautions and Conclusions*, 10.

[26] Craig Ott, "Missionary Methods: The Questions That Still Dog Us," in *Missionary Methods: Research, Reflections and Realities*, 195.

[27] Payne, in *Missionary Methods: Research, Reflections and Realities*, xvi.

and mission theory is an interdisciplinary process that integrates, to varying degrees, these three main fields: (1) the Bible, biblical studies, theology, and church beliefs and creeds; (2) mission biography, history of mission, missionary experience, and missionary methods; and (3) social and behavioural sciences. This is shown in Table 3.

Missiologist	Method	Components
Tippett	Mission fills an in-between position	Theology, theory, and history of mission and anthropology
Hesselgrave	Types of source materials for missional inquiry, research, and reflection	Bible, church beliefs/creeds, and related theological methodology, social and behavioural sciences, mission biography, and history
Pocock	Integrated system for missiological study	Theology, missionary experience, social sciences
Ott	Interdisciplinary subjects for study of missional methods	Theology, mission history, social science
Payne	Foundations for study of missional theory	Base: theology and biblical studies; Middle: missiology; Top: missionary methods

Table 3: Components of Missiological Methodology

Theoretical Categories of Mission Theology

To deepen our comprehension of Mission Theology, let us explore this through four lenses, each from a different mission theologian. Each lens provides an insight into the complexities and simplicities of mission and strengthens a comprehensive understanding of Mission Theology.

Cathy Ross draws on work by the Anglican Consultative Council in the 1980–1990s who developed a framework defined by five aspects they called 'marks':

1. 'To proclaim the Good News of the Kingdom [Mark 1:15, Luke 4:18].
2. To teach, baptize, and nurture new believers [Matt. 28:18-20].
3. To respond to human needs by loving service [Matt. 22:34-40].
4. To seek to transform unjust structures of society [Matt. 6:33, Micah 6:8].
5. To strive to safeguard the integrity of creation and sustain and renew the life of the earth [Ps. 24:1, Col. 1:15-20].'[28]

These marks give a simple yet 'holistic approach to mission'.[29] The marks are comprehensive in that mission is not intended to be just one or two of the marks, such as proclaiming the good news, or teaching, baptising, and nurturing new believers. The marks give guidance to 'engage in God's mission in your corner

---

[28] Cathy Ross, "Introduction: *Taonga*," in *Mission in the 21st Century: Exploring the Five Marks of Global Mission*, ed. Andrew Walls and Cathy Ross (Maryknoll: Orbis Books, 2008), xiv.

[29] Ross, in *Mission in the 21st Century: Exploring the Five Marks of Global Mission*, xiv.

of the world – the world not only as we have made it, scarred with compromise, but also the world that belongs to God and is alive with potential' because of who God is and his love for all his creation.[30]

Charles Van Engen places God's mission into seven foundational categories with grand Latin names (in Western theology, placing labels in Latin makes them seem more impressive!).[31] These foundations are broad categories that show the breadth of God's missional plan and are seen in Table 4.

Categories of Mission Theory	God's Missional Action
Missio Dei	The Mission of God
Missio Hominum	Missional Use of Human Agents
Missiones Ecclesiarum	Missions Through the Corporate People of God [i.e. the church]
Missio Politica Oecumenica	Missional Action in Global Civilization
Missio Christi	Messianic Mission Through Jesus Christ
Missio Espiritu Sancti	Mission Through the Holy Spirit
Missio Futurum / Adventus	Kingdom Mission in the Predictable Future and Surprising Advent

Table 4: Categories of God's Missional Action

Kwame Bediako offers a Mission Research Taxonomy with seven categories as an interdisciplinary approach to study and evaluate the impact of mission in various contexts. The model has four overlapping components (numbered 1 to 4) along with three underlying and binding aspects shown in Diagram 4.[32]

---

[30] Ross, in *Mission in the 21st Century: Exploring the Five Marks of Global Mission*, xv.

[31] Van Engen, 174–75.

[32] Kwame Bediako, "The African Renaissance and Theological Reconstruction: The Challenge of the Twenty-First Century," *Journal of African Christian Thought* 4, no. 2 (2001): 29–33.

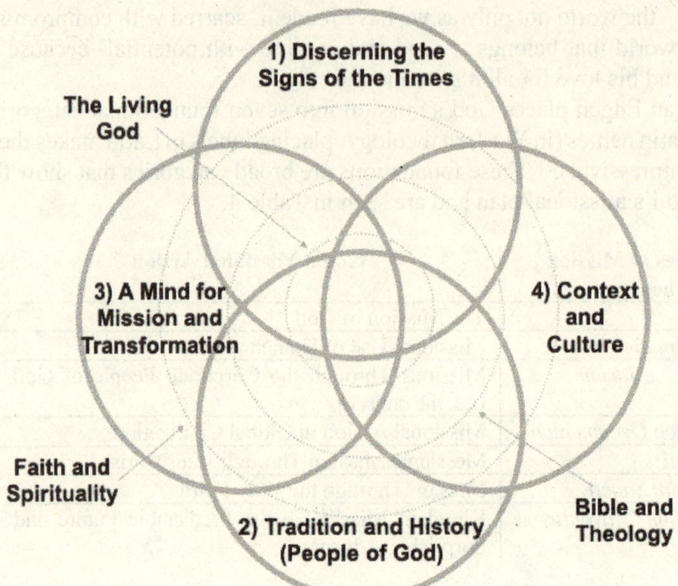

Diagram 4: Mission Research Taxonomy

The principle of the model is that mission research will lie in one or more of the seven fields of study. Most mission research occurs in the interface between the four major components and the three underlying aspects. Mission research seeks to discern how the triune God is at work in his mission. The details of this model are given below.

Overarching Fields of Mission Study and Research

1. **Discerning the Signs of the Times:** The starting point to explore what is significant at the given historical moment and what God is doing at this time. The process considers factors, forces, problems, issues, questions people face, and responses to all of these factors and motives (conversion, civilisation, discipleship, church planting, justice, reign of God, and colonial/postcolonial ethics).
2. **Tradition and History (People of God):** Discernment of the times requires connection with the wider Christian history and tradition. The process considers the history of missions, geography, churches, global, regional, and thematic gatherings, cross-cultural missionaries, local agents, models of mission, mission methods and techniques, well-equipped specialist mission agencies, multifaceted partnerships, specialised agencies, and vocational approaches (health, education, agriculture, community development, BAM, creation care).
3. **A Mind for Mission and Transformation:** An appreciation of how knowledge, intellectual activity, and participation in God's mission are

bound to spiritual discipleship. The process considers strategies and tactics for mission, including mission agencies, mission NGOs, leadership development and training, mission and vocational approaches to mission, evangelism and church planting, discipleship, worship and ethnomusicology, interreligious dialogue, holistic mission, communication techniques (radio, online, publishing), partnership and collaboration, church planting, growth and renewal, evaluation, and reporting.

4. **Context and Culture:** The cultural context over time offers changes that may negatively or positively inform developments in the modern setting. The process considers how the gospel engages with religions/culture, intercultural mission studies, migration, world religions, other worldviews, comparative religion, mission and language, local theologising, anthropology, gender, identity, mission and society, integral mission, justice and compassion, and discipleship.

Underlying Binding Aspects

The Living God: Indigenous experience of God, the Trinity, and manifestations and forms; *missio Dei*, reign/kingdom of God, *shalom*, Great Commission, missional hermeneutic, and faithful witness.

Bible and Theology: Biblical studies, theology of mission, theology of religion, contextual theology, mission and ecclesiology, mission and eschatology, mission and pneumatology, and mission and ecology.

Faith and Spirituality: Differing spiritualities, worldview and Christian confession, and spirituality and mission.

John Flett brings us back to basics. He notes that despite 50 years of theological reflection on the *missio Dei*, there is still a 'lack of cohesion' and coordination concerning the essential elements of mission. He gives a more straightforward framework placing all of mission – its marks, foundational categories, and complexity of human activity – covered above into these three elements of mission that he states form the *missio Dei*:

(1) its Trinitarian basis;

(2) its orientation towards the kingdom of God;

(3) its human instrumentality – the 'missionary nature of the church'.[33]

Integrative Missiological Matrix

Charles Van Engen also provides a missiological framework of interacting disciplines of Mission Theology that, when used in an engaging-reflecting manner, serves as that gadfly that David Bosch writes about. Bosch describes missiology as a 'gadfly' to all that is mission, which 'persistently annoy[s] or provoke[s] others with criticism, schemes, ideas, demands [and] requests'.[34] For

---

[33] John Flett, *The Witness of God: The Trinity, Missio Dei, Karl Barth, and the Nature of Christian Community* (Grand Rapids: Wm B Eerdmans, 2010), 76.

[34] Gadfly," accessed 20 May 2022, https://www.dictionary.com/browse/gadfly.

Bosch, a gadfly 'accompan[ies] the missionary enterprise, to scrutinize its foundations, aims, attitude, message, and methods'… and questions the status quo.[35]

Van Engen's approach is helpful, using the following sources to inform missional reflection and practice in the *missio Dei*: Bible, Church, Personal Pilgrimage, and Context. To Van Engen's list, we add another factor – Praxis, thus encompassing practical application. These sources all integrate and co-occur, providing a view of the whole while simultaneously considering the unique contribution of each.[36] We have adapted Van Engen's model and call this an Integrative Missiological Matrix. Its main components are illustrated in Diagram 5.

Diagram 5: Integrative Missiological Matrix

Let's now look at the main components.

In the ***Missio Dei,*** God is engaged in, and the source of mission for, the salvation activity of the triune missionary God, because this is an attribute of the triune God, particularly his sending love. God's mission belongs to him. God extends the gift of salvation to all people and the establishment of the Lordship of Christ over all redeemed creation.

The ***Bible*** is the exclusive source text for theologising about God's mission (*missio Dei*), the revelation of the missionary God, and the inbreaking of God into human history. The Bible, interpreted through a missional hermeneutic, provides the boundary that informs, shapes, and critiques the other domains.

The ***Church*** is the primary agent of God's mission into the world. Its theological and missiological reflection about its understanding of God's

---

[35] Bosch, *Transforming Mission: Paradigm Shifts in Theology of Mission*, 496.
[36] Van Engen, 25–27.

mission over time serves as its biography, historical development, and contribution.

Personal Pilgrimage encompasses our journey as the human agent of God's mission, including our spiritual gifts, natural abilities, experiences, knowledge, and personality, influencing how God's mission is incarnated through each person's life. This domain affects how the other sources are interpreted and understood.

Contexts are the unique environments and perspectives of the world where God's mission occurs. These include culture, socio-economics, political realities, and other areas of human life. Mission action and reflection need to be contextually appropriate. The social sciences (e.g. sociology, anthropology, psychology, economics, and urbanology) provide the tools to understand and engage in the contexts of mission.

Mission Theology helps us understand and participate more effectively in the *missio Dei*. Mission Theology is interested in the assumptions and underlying principles which determine the Christian faith in terms of the motivation, message, methods, strategies, and goals of Christian mission.

Praxis has the function of ensuring a robust engagement between action and reflection in the *missio Dei*. Praxis ensures this action–reflection process occurs continually. Mission praxis helps mission practitioners maintain a healthy balance between focusing primarily on mission activities or actions and providing an ongoing process for missional reflection that better informs this practice.

There is a secondary level of the the Integrated Missiological Framework illustrated in Diagram 6.

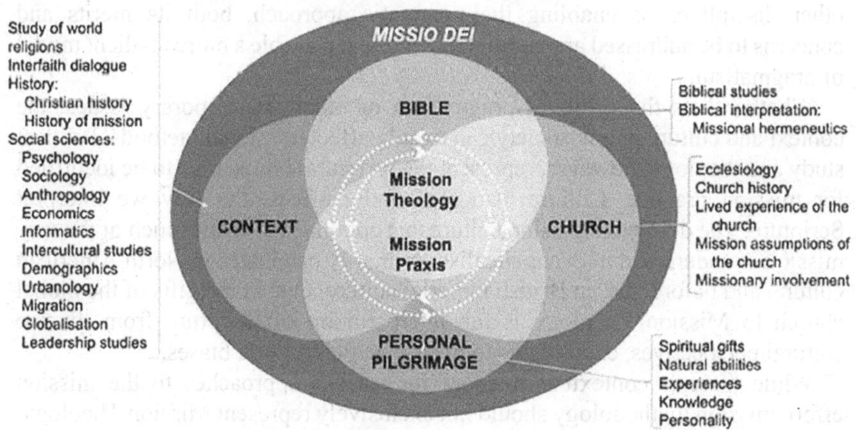

Diagram 6: Application of Integrative Missiological Matrix

In the Integrative Missiological Matrix are functions that help in considering and exploring participation in God's mission. For example, with ***Bible***, biblical studies and biblical interpretation, especially missional hermeneutics, are methods to probe God's intentions for his mission. Associated with ***Church*** are ecclesiology, church history, the church's assumptions of mission, and how it has lived out those functions through its missionary involvement. Under ***Personal Pilgrimage***, the inner life of individuals participating in God's mission includes personality, knowledge, experiences, natural abilities, and spiritual gifts for serving. Finally, under ***Context***, many disciplines associated with social sciences, Christian and mission history, studying other religions and interfaith dialogue are helpful in studying and understanding God's mission. These components are not exhaustive but aid in making sense of the complexities of God's mission and our participation in it.

Applying Mission Theory to Mission Practice

Reflecting on pragmatism and its theoretical underpinnings reveals the significance of its effect on mission practice. Pragmatism as a theoretical model supports using whatever method works to achieve the desired outcome. Its development can be traced to the Age of Enlightenment and rationalism, and its fulfilment can be found in North American business practices. Pragmatism has profoundly affected how evangelicals in the late twentieth century have approached and engaged in mission, including the extraordinary focus on methods used to ensure the church's numerical growth, often excluding or overlooking the contribution of the interdisciplinary perspective of Mission Theology. By studying pragmatism in mission through the lens of Mission Theology and considering biblical texts, mission history, anthropology, and other disciplines as enabling the pragmatic approach, both its merits and concerns to be addressed are highlighted, making possible a more resilient model of pragmatism.

Whether it is the result of pragmatism or other contemporary issues, the context and culture of any society can unduly affect missional methods. Biblical study and theology, however, represent the scriptural boundaries to be identified for mission practice. Culture also profoundly affects the way we interpret Scripture. The dominant mission culture that continues to shape much of the way mission is understood in evangelicalism primarily originates in North American culture, and before that, in British imperial culture. One of the gifts of the global church to Mission Theology is the interpretation of Scripture from diverse cultural perspectives, enabling us to overcome our cultural biases.

While there is contextual freedom for various approaches to the mission effort, mission methodology should not exclusively represent Mission Theology. An ongoing and healthy interchange between theory and practice is necessary, each affecting the other. Theory informs praxis, and reflection on experience, in turn, influences our theoretical understanding.

Global, regional, and local contexts are continually in flux. Globalisation and the increasing rate of change require that methodologies adapt and adjust.

Missional practice must rely on something other than previously effective or successful methods.

Developing a theological understanding of mission involves integrating reflection and practice and calls for mission practitioners and theorists to identify those concerns in mission most in need of urgent attention. Pursuing best practices that are both effective and biblically based, missional practice must be subjected to an ongoing appraisal.

Some methods may have a short lifespan, while others may be indefinite. When change is called for, mission practitioners must have the courage to adjust in light of, and without compromising, biblical insights or integrity.

Western Mission Issues

Mission researchers, without adequate theological reflection, have not always provided helpful guidance about developments in mission. The task of the mission theologian is to explore a fresh understanding of Scripture in light of changing contexts, considering history, the reality of the church, and our own experiences. Mission issues and questions should be re-examined because they will perpetually be at the forefront of mission research and practice. Michael Goheen, as a Western missiologist, offers this list of issues to consider:

- *Missional hermeneutics:* Renewed understanding of mission through a fresh study of the whole counsel of God (i.e. the Bible).
- *Mission history:* A review of the mission history from its Western bias.
- *Nature of mission:* Reflection of the mission of the triune God in today's world.
- *Contextualisation*: How the Christian faith relates to the contexts that surround it.
- *The gospel:* How globalisation has been an agent of spreading Western values.
- *Encounter with other world religions*: The relationship of Christian mission with other faith communities.
- *Urban mission*: How mission takes place in urban areas.[37]

Topics Needing Majority World Perspectives

A significant challenge facing the developers of mission theory is how theorists and practitioners from the Majority World interrelate and collaborate in mission research with their counterparts. How can these voices bring new perspectives and understandings into the whole church? These are some examples of where these perspectives are needed in the context of international missions:

- *National identity:* Supporting aspirations of national leaders to develop how local ownership of ministry fits, flourishes, and functions within international mission agencies.

---

[37] Michael Goheen, *Introducing Christian Mission Today: Scripture, History and Issues* (Downers Grove: IVP Academic, 2014), 27–31.

• *Leadership:* Acknowledging wrongs made, asking for forgiveness, and restoring relationships in authentic reconciliation requires humility, listening more to God and one another, and learning together.

• *Partnering and collaborating:* Developing relationships through greater dependence on God and each other with intentionality to strengthen commitment, vulnerability, and trust.

• *Resource sharing:* Recognising the interdependent relational activity where all participants and their contributions are valued, each can graciously give and receive, and the dignity of all is honoured through mutually respectful friendships.

A Caution

Due to its diverse interpretation and application, recognising and conveying what makes up mission present a challenging and ongoing proposition. Consequently, Gary Tyra refers to the *missio Dei* as an 'elastic concept' that continuously integrates new meanings.[38] While God's actions are wide-ranging, some aspects do not change, such as 'his relational, self-giving, grace-filled nature'.[39] Flett refers to this challenge as 'a bog of elasticity' because, despite its Trinitarian basis, *missio Dei* always has 'anthropological grounding'.[40]

The expanding theological discussion about mission is dynamic. David Bosch describes mission as 'multidimensional'. It covers a broad spectrum that includes 'witness, service, justice, healing, reconciliation, liberation, peace, evangelism, fellowship, church planting, contextualization, and much more', and should not be defined too narrowly.[41] Stephen Neill warns, 'if everything is mission, then nothing is mission'.[42] Christopher Wright gives a different perspective, of what he describes as a 'more biblical perspective to say, "If everything is mission… everything is mission"' because 'everything a Christian and a Christian church is, says, and does should be missional in its conscious participation in the mission of God in God's world'.[43] Nonetheless, Andrew Kirk is cautious as he suggests that defining mission, if left unconstrained, could lead to its loss of significance and its being undervalued, and contribute to simplistic mission catchphrases.[44]

---

[38] Tyra, 310.

[39] Emma Wild-Wood, and Peniel Rajkumar, *Foundations for Mission* (Oxford: Regnum, 2013), 290.

[40] Flett, 76.

[41] Bosch, *Transforming Mission: Paradigm Shifts in Theology of Mission*, 512.

[42] Stephen Neill, *Creative Tension: The Duff Lectures* (London: Edinburgh House Press, 1959), 81.

[43] Christopher Wright, *The Mission of God's People* (Grand Rapids: Zondervan, 2010), 26.

[44] Kirk, 25.

Summary

We began this chapter with the idea that God's mission describes his plan for everyone and everything to be brought together under the Lordship of Christ. We noted how Mission Theology is a multidisciplinary study and is integral rather than peripheral to all of theology. It questions, clarifies, integrates, and expands the assumptions of those various related disciplines. Today's global mission contexts require mission practitioners and theorists to identify important topics for missiological study and reflection. In this process, we can draw from principles, methods, and frameworks for effective foundations and practices in mission. These principles, methods, and frameworks created by seasoned missiologists remind us of how Mission Theology is as rich and varied as the ingredients that comprise it.

The constantly changing contexts locally, regionally, and globally involve adjusting and changing mission methodologies. The implication is that missional praxis must rely on more than just working strategies from the past. Some methods may have a short lifespan, while others may be indefinite. When change is necessary, missional practitioners must have the courage to adjust without compromising biblical insights or integrity. Therefore, across the globe, we should always search for best practices that are biblically based, effective, and subject to ongoing appraisal.

Reflective Questions:

- What other mission-related topics would you add that need exploration by Western and/or Majority World mission theorists and practitioners?
- How can our adaptation of Charles Van Engen's Integrative Missiological Matrix lead to a fuller understanding of mission's breadth, complexity, and possibility?

6. Biblical and Theological Road Map

Introduction

There are many methods and pathways to approach and interpret the biblical text. Theologians call this hermeneutics – the science of interpreting the Scriptures.[1] Christopher Wright states, 'the mission of God provides a valid hermeneutical framework or a trustworthy map for the journey of biblical understanding' about the *missio Dei*.[2]

Wright and a growing group of other scholars have developed methods of studying mission throughout the whole of the Bible. This methodology is called a missional hermeneutic (or an approach of interpreting the biblical text through Mission Theology). According to Craig Ott, this interpretive approach has been considered 'an overlooked way, and it must be recovered'.[3] Mission Theology is not only simply about concepts and ideas – it must also be grounded in Scripture. Mission Theology's foundations are the whole revelation of God. How we interpret biblical texts will be critical for understanding Mission Theology.

Missional Hermeneutics

Mark Simon states that a missional reading of Scripture depends on the 'explicit faith in the biblical narrative as God's word given to form the believing community for participation in God's mission in the world'.[4] Sung Chan Kwon notes reading Scripture this way is 'valid because (1) the Bible as a whole reveals the mission of God and (2) the Bible has been produced in missional circumstances'.[5] Recognising the complete scriptural text as the revelation of God's mission, Wright notes, 'a missional hermeneutic proceeds from the assumption that *the whole Bible renders to us the story of God's mission through God's people in their engagement with God's world for the sake of God's purpose for the whole of God's creation.*'[6] Simon outlines the main features of this hermeneutic:

- 'It is a lens specifically designed to investigate mission in the Bible;
- It takes a broad view of what constitutes mission, not limiting it to initial evangelism through verbal proclamation;

---

[1] Hermeneutics," accessed 20 February 2022, https://www.dictionary.com/browse/hermeneutics.

[2] Christopher Wright, *The Mission of God: Unlocking the Bible's Grand Narrative* (Downers Grove: IVP Academic, 2006), 532.

[3] Craig Ott, *The Church on Mission: A Biblical Vision for Transformation among All People* (Grand Rapids: Baker Academic, 2019), 52.

[4] Simon, 27.

[5] Kwon, 22.

[6] Wright, 51.

- It provides a set of questions that invites deeper investigation of mission from multiple perspectives;
- It is oriented towards contemporary relevance in addition to historical analysis;
- It seeks to enrich biblical scholarship through incorporating insights and concerns from the field of missiology.'[7]

This is an integrated way of recognising that Mission Theology is based on an awareness that Scripture in its entirety speaks to us of the mission of God and how we participate in it. Rather than limiting us, this draws us towards the richness of the missiological threads running throughout Scripture. Bible passages may sometimes be interpreted differently, depending on the context. When we interpret Scripture within the framework of our context, new understandings of the *missio Dei* emerge because the Bible holds 'multiple layers of meaning'.[8]

Craig Ott sees the benefit of reading the biblical text with a missional hermeneutic. This methodology helps us 'contextualize the application of the Bible, to identify the missional thrust of the Bible, and to locate ourselves in the story of Scripture and redemptive history'.[9] This requires taking the study of the Bible seriously, as Ott states, 'not flippantly', as one who 'discount[s] the value of theological reflection and education'.[10]

Paul Zilonka and Michael Gorman elaborate that 'when we interpret the Bible from the perspective of faith, even from an academic point of view, we [treat] it as Scripture, as sacred text – not merely as ancient literature'.[11] Reading Scripture with mission as our primary interest, we are wise to consider Michael Goheen's insight that it is 'relatively uncommon to see biblical scholarship take seriously the insights of missiology' (or Mission Theology).[12]

The same Spirit who inspired the human writers of the Scriptures is alive and at work in our world and in us today. It is that Spirit who brings Scripture alive in our context. Different contexts help us understand Scripture and God's mission differently. Whether we live in poverty or affluence, religious pluralism or secularism, these gifts help cultivate a deeper, fuller comprehension of God's mission in the world. As we focus on specific Scriptures or engage in certain issues and contextual questions, we must also-include the Scriptures – what God is saying to us today – to facilitate our understanding of Mission Theology.

---

[7] Simon, 27.

[8] Balia, and Kim, 23.

[9] Ott, *The Church on Mission: A Biblical Vision for Transformation Among All People*, 54.

[10] Ott, *The Church on Mission: A Biblical Vision for Transformation Among All People*, 54.

[11] Paul, Zilonka, and Michael Gorman. "The Bible: A Book, a Library, a Story, an Invitation," in *Scripture and Its Interpretation*, ed. Michael Gorman (Grand Rapids: Baker Academic, 2017, Kindle edition), 580.

[12] Michael Goheen, "A History and Introduction to a Missional Reading of the Bible," in Reading the Bible Missionally, ed. Michael Goheen (Wm. B. Eerdmans Publishing: Grand Rapids, 2016, Kindle edition), 156.

Michael Goheen states, 'mission is a central category in the Bible that needs to be taken seriously if our interpretation is to be faithful'.[13] The challenge for the study of Mission Theology is to acknowledge and respect the 'rich diversity' of the biblical text and not 'reduce [our] biblical foundation for mission to a single word, idea, or text as the unifying hermeneutic lens through which to see Scripture'.[14]

Hermeneutic Matrix

Dean Flemming suggests there is 'no consensus' on what 'a missional reading of Scripture' looks like, but importantly, there is agreement that it is not limited to Bible passages often categorised as referring to mission, such as Matthew 28, Acts 1, etc.[15] Many texts attempt to bring clarity to this topic. For instance, *Reading the Bible Missionally* with Michael Goheen as editor gives examples from the Old and New Testaments that approach the biblical texts through a Mission Theology interpretation. Dean Flemming, a contributor in that book, quoting from George Hunsberger, identifies four methods for missional hermeneutics: (1) reading 'Scripture as a witness to the gracious mission of the triune God'; (2) asking 'how the biblical writings function to equip and energise God's people to participate in the *missio Dei*'; (3) showing 'particular interest in the missional location of the communities reading Scripture and the questions those communities bring to the text'; and (4) emphasising 'Scripture's missional engagement with different cultures and social contexts, in light of the Christ-centered gospel'.[16]

Goheen has four streams of a missional hermeneutic that, when used, 'provide a broad and innovative approach to biblical interpretation'.[17] They are: (1) 'Mission as the theme of the Bible': consider how specific texts declare God's mission of redemption and reconciliation; (2) 'Equipping for mission': reflect upon 'the purpose of the Bible as *a tool to equip* God's people for mission'; (3) 'Missional locatedness of the readers': consider the place in God's mission of the present-day 'reader'; and (4) 'Missional engagement with culture': study 'how the received biblical tradition is critically brought to bear on particular cultural contexts'.[18]

Mark Simon identifies critical features of missional hermeneutics, starting with David Bosch's call for 'reading the entire Bible missiologically'.[19] Simon

---

[13] Goheen, 156.

[14] Goheen, 199.

[15] Dean Flemming, "A Missional Reading of Colossians," in *Reading the Bible Missionally*, ed. Michael Goheen (Grand Rapids: Wm B. Eerdmans, 2016), 213.

[16] Flemming, in *Reading the Bible Missionally*, 213.

[17] Michael Goheen, *A Light to the Nations: The Missional Church and the Biblical Story* (Grand Rapids: Baker Academic, 2011), 35.

[18] Goheen, *A Light to the Nations: The Missional Church and the Biblical Story*, 30, 33, 34.

[19] Simon, 28.

uses Hunsberger's observation of the biblical text's interrelationship with the 'reader's circumstances… for the hermeneutical process'.[20]

Sung Chan Kwon starts with William Carey's use of Matthew 28 as a biblical basis for mission. He ends with Bosch's four features of the Old and the New Testament's 'missional significance', namely: 'compassion, history, suffering, and conduct'.[21] Kwon offers these insights into a missional hermeneutic: (1) it 'is an unassuming process of reading the text itself rather than a deductive process of reading mission into the given text'[22]; (2) 'the Bible as a whole reveals the mission of God'; (3) 'the Bible has been produced in missional circumstances'[23]; and (4) using John's gospel as an example, it 'could be viewed as a product of the Evangelist's self-reflection… The example provides a guideline for a church, in any given context, to begin the selfhood and self-theologizing process'.[24]

Combining the observations of Flemming, Goheen, and Kwon, we have a matrix of the main values of missional hermeneutics, as seen in Table 5. Each perspective is helpful, and used together provides a comprehensive missional hermeneutic framework.

Flemming	Goheen	Kwon
Reading Scripture as a witness to the gracious mission of the triune God	Mission as the theme of the Bible	The entire Bible reveals the mission of God
Asking how the biblical writings function to equip and energise God's people to participate in the *missio Dei*	Equipping for mission	The unassuming process of reading the text itself rather than a deductive process of reading mission into the given text
Showing particular interest in the missional location of the communities reading Scripture and the questions those communities bring to the text	Missional locatedness of the readers	The Bible has been produced in missional circumstances
Emphasising Scripture's missional engagement with different cultures and social contexts because of the Christ-centred gospel	Missional engagement with culture	Self-reflection of the biblical authors provides a guideline in any context to a self-theologising process

Table 5: Comparison of Missional Hermeneutics

---

[20] Simon, 30.
[21] Kwon, 18.
[22] Kwon, 27.
[23] Kwon, 22.
[24] Kwon, 188.

Hermeneutic Examples

Let us now look at some examples of missional hermeneutics offered by missiologists and theologians. Dean Flemming shows a two-fold approach to reading Paul's letter to the Colossians as (1) 'a *witness* to the mission of God and the people who are caught up in that mission'; and (2) 'an *instrument* of the *missio Dei*'.[25] This reading 'takes seriously how Paul contextualizes the gospel for his first-century audience, within their particular life circumstances'.[26] Some examples of Flemming's missional hermeneutic of Colossians are:

- *Missional setting:* 'Paul writes as missionary-pastor to a young Christian congregation... in Colossae... for the Colossians to live as a mature, stable, missional community, faithful to the Christ they received (1:23-28; 2:6-7; 4:5-6).' There was a syncretistic 'rival "philosophy" threatening the gospel'.[27]

- *Missional strategy:* Paul 'reflect[s] positively on the gospel of God's redemptive mission in Christ' (1:5-6).[28]

- *Missional starting point:* Rather than God's mission beginning with the Fall, Colossians positions it as starting with creation by focusing on 'Christ's role in creation and reconciliation [and his] relationship to the creation, the world, and the powers' (1:15-20).[29]

- *Missional ending point:* The Colossians can 'embrace a forward-looking *hope*, kept for them in heaven (1:5), promised in the gospel (1:23), and belonging to the reality of future glory (1:27, cf. 3:4)'.[30]

- *Missional purpose:* 'Paul's mission [regarding] the Colossians is that they remain stable and firmly established in the faith (1:23)' and 'that they might have the full riches of complete understanding, so that they may know the mystery of God, namely, Christ, in whom are hidden all the treasures of wisdom and knowledge' (2:2-3, NIV).[31]

- *Missional identity:* Paul desires the Colossians to understand the 'superiority and sufficiency of Christ' that helps them form 'a faithful, mature, missional community' (1:2, 3:12-17).[32]

- *Missional community:* 'Paul energizes the church to participate in God's mission [by reminding] them that they are part of something much bigger than themselves' (1:5-6, 3:11, 1:20).[33]

- *Missional message:* Paul addresses how 'God's people should relate to unbelievers' (3:5–4:6) with the missional implications of 'a witness of word and a witness of life'.[34]

---

[25] Flemming, in *Reading the Bible Missionally*, 214.
[26] Flemming, in *Reading the Bible Missionally*, 214.
[27] Flemming, in *Reading the Bible Missionally*, 214.
[28] Flemming, in *Reading the Bible Missionally*, 216.
[29] Flemming, in *Reading the Bible Missionally*, 217.
[30] Flemming, in *Reading the Bible Missionally*, 222.
[31] Flemming, in *Reading the Bible Missionally*, 224.
[32] Flemming, in *Reading the Bible Missionally*, 225.
[33] Flemming, in *Reading the Bible Missionally*, 226.
[34] Flemming, in *Reading the Bible Missionally*, 231.

Flemming's reading of Colossians shows how Paul was concerned about forming 'a mature, missional congregation in Colossae' and how 'this letter can *continue* to equip Christian communities to participate in God's mission today'.[35] Importantly, a

> missional reading of Colossians, then, seeks to understand how this Christ-exalting letter bears witness to God's all-embracing mission in the world and how it calls Christian communities to engage in that mission in their own corners of the world… Like the early Christians of the Lycus Valley, we live out our missional identity simultaneously 'in Christ' and 'in Colossae' (1:2). We, too, must resist the temptation to let an overdose of 'Colossae' cloud our Christian identity and witness. And like them, it is precisely 'in Colossae' that we embody God's mission, speaking and living the gospel in the presence of a watching world (4:5-6).[36]

Mark Simon gives another example of a missional hermeneutic. He surveys Ephesians to determine whether there is any merit to some scholars' claims that Paul's letter is 'uninterested in mission'.[37] Simon studies this epistle for its 'portrayal of the *missio Dei*'[38] through a comprehensive process of examining 'intertextual links to mission in the wider biblical narrative' and 'the portrayal of Paul and his involvement in mission'.[39] Simon hypothesises that 'Ephesians is a missional document' with the purpose 'to inform, encourage and shape its recipients for participation' in God's mission.[40]

Proof-texting is a concern for Simon. For example, it is typical for 'biblical theologies of mission' to refer to Ephesians 'as a proof text for a particular theme such as reconciliation or spiritual powers'.[41] Another usage finds 'individual proof texts from their literary contexts' and applies them to 'broader missional principles or themes'.[42]

The structure Simon applies to the nine pericopes of the epistle 'based on UBS [United Bible Societies] divisions of the text'[43] includes an introduction (overview of missional categories); the *missio Dei*'s implications; a portrayal of God's person and character; intertextuality (the links of the pericope to other biblical narratives); how humanity and the world are portrayed in God's mission; evidence of a missional context concerning the problems, crises, or issues being addressed; and how Paul is depicted with his participation in God's mission. Exploring intertextuality, Simon looks for relationships between sections of Ephesians 'and the wider biblical text' following Richard Hays' 'tests for echoes' (e.g. 'metalepsis') of Old Testament 'material' in the Ephesians text.[44]

---

[35] Flemming, in *Reading the Bible Missionally*, 232.
[36] Flemming, in *Reading the Bible Missionally*, 238.
[37] Simon, 2.
[38] Simon, xiv.
[39] Simon, xiv.
[40] Simon, 3.
[41] Simon, 15.
[42] Simon, 18.
[43] Simon, 44.
[44] Simon, 42.

Examples of Simon's analysis of Ephesians:

• Under the intertextuality of 1:15-23, comparisons are made with 1 Thessalonians 1:3-10, and Simon observes, 'the transformation of lives due to the gospel is therefore both an outcome of mission and a foundation for the ongoing missional life of communities'.[45]

• In 2:11-22, under the category of *missio Dei*, Simon notes that reconciliation is 'a powerful missional concept [and] lies at the heart of this passage'.[46]

• Through how humanity and the world are portrayed in God's mission, Simon refers to 3:10, noting 'the church is missional by… its worship and community life, rather than solely through verbal proclamation'.[47]

• In 6:10-20, Simon notes the portrayal of 'the *missio Dei* as involving a spiritual struggle against evil powers and principalities. God has equipped believers to prevail in this struggle'.[48]

Simon's thorough exploration of Ephesians to see whether it is a missional document illustrates that missional readings of the letter have 'not been analysed consistently or comprehensively'.[49] Simon corrects this by meticulously exploring mission in every pericope of the book. Simon proves the letter is not 'inward-focused'.[50] Instead, missional themes include 'ethical and verbal witness to the nations'.[51] Simon assures his readers that the letter upholds a 'consistent and coherent concern for mission' and the '*missio Dei* [is] elucidated in every pericope'.[52]

As another example, Sung Chan Kwon's work of a missional reading of John's gospel is 'an assuming process of reading the text itself rather than a deductive process of reading mission into the given text'.[53] Kwon follows two approaches for doing this: (1) drawing from the canonical setting to see how this serves a missional understanding; and (2) how Jesus forms his disciples to participate in God's mission. Kwon applies this missional hermeneutic through four pericopes.

Kwon notes that the missional portrayal of sending is a characteristic of John's gospel: 'the purpose of the sending should be found through the whole narrative'.[54] Finding the right balance in interpreting the sending theme concerns Kwon. He notes how recent interpretations of *missio Dei* overstate 'the action of sending compared to the other aspects of God's character'.[55] To insist that the *missio Dei* is based on the 'sending aspect' of the doctrine of the Trinity is what

---

[45] Simon, 68.

[46] Simon, 95.

[47] Simon, 139.

[48] Simon, 216.

[49] Simon, 44.

[50] Simon, 252.

[51] Simon, 252.

[52] Simon, 252.

[53] Kwon, 27.

[54] Kwon, 9.

[55] Kwon, 173.

Kwon calls 'a "proof-doctrine" or "missionary-doctrine" approach to mission'.[56] Instead, sending is based on 'the relationship and oneness between the Father and the Son and knowing the will of the Father in the relationship'.[57] The missional implication of the divine relational dimension of the triune God is the foundation for sending the discipleship community.

The new discipleship community is a theme that Kwon traces through his reading of John's gospel. For example, 'the incarnate Word, Jesus, formed a discipleship community', and this new community reflects 'the "being together" of the Word with God' (1:37–51).[58] The new community has 'its mission to the world' (1:1–2:12).[59] This new community is a 'discipleship community [that] is also missional' because 'God is missional' (2:13–12:50).[60] Jesus prays for his followers and waits for them to 'be a believing discipleship community' (13:1–17:26).[61] 'Believing in Jesus means belonging to the triune God's community and, at the same time, to the discipleship community' (16:27).[62] 'The mission of the discipleship community is based on their loving relationship with the Lord rather than on their own passion, and the ministry is owned by the Lord rather than by themselves' (21:19).[63] The formation of this new community is critical and prominent for a missional reading of John's gospel because it 'is a priority of Jesus' ministry, according to the Gospel'.[64] Kwon concludes that 'mission is the full engagement of the discipleship community, rather than merely delegated work to specific forces within the community'.[65]

Through these missional hermeneutic examples, we see how Flemming's reading of Colossians, Simon's exploration of Ephesians, and Kwon's analysis of the fourth gospel provide missional concepts and themes from three New Testament books. For a more comprehensive work that approaches the entire Bible through a missional hermeneutic lens, one should consult Christopher Wright. He states that a 'missional hermeneutic of the Bible begins with the Bible's very existence' and 'the whole canon of Scripture is a missional phenomenon in the sense that it witnesses to the self-giving movement of this God toward his creation and us, human beings in God's image, but wayward and wanton. The writings that now comprise our Bible are themselves the product of and witness to the ultimate mission of God.'[66]

When considering a missional hermeneutic, we must not limit ourselves to the New Testament. Wright explains: 'The Old Testament tells its story as the story or, rather, as a part of that ultimate and universal story that will ultimately

---

[56] Kwon, 173.

[57] Kwon, 179.

[58] Kwon, 64.

[59] Kwon, 76.

[60] Kwon, 105.

[61] Kwon, 129.

[62] Kwon, 153.

[63] Kwon, 156.

[64] Kwon, 166.

[65] Kwon, 188.

[66] Wright, 48.

embrace the whole of creation, time, and humanity within its scope.'[67] Wright calls this a 'metanarrative' or a 'grand narrative'.[68]

As an Old Testament example, Tim Davy applies a missional reading to the Book of Job because it offers abundant and captivating material for contemplating the mission of God. It brings forth valuable insights and addresses mission-related questions in a unique and significant way. Themes that Davy explores include how 'the book could be considered as a "missional encounter" with the surrounding cultures'.[69] Davy observes how the biblical text interacts with and challenges the perspectives and ideologies of neighbouring cultures in Israel's context.[70] Another missional theme is that 'sustained and probing examination of unattributed suffering is part of Scripture'.[71] Davy notes how these 'intense human experiences' are shown through 'Israelite sages' in an 'international conversation on suffering' and offer 'a probing of the issue that is shaped by faith in Yahweh'.[72] This survey of suffering signifies Yahweh's deep concern for the universal human experience of pain, thus compelling the church to honestly confront this issue.[73]

Another significant theme that Davy unwraps in the text is poverty and the treatment of the poor. He frames this within holistic mission, which he calls a 'significant motif in the book of Job itself'.[74] Davy notes how the 'descriptions of the plight and (mis-) treatment of the poor, plays an important role in the development of the book of Job, and especially from Job's perspective as he seeks to question his circumstances and achieve vindication'.[75]

Wright notes that there is no one set methodology for a missional hermeneutic, and therefore, one needs to recognise 'the multiplicity of perspectives and contexts from which and within which people read the biblical texts [because] the plurality of perspectives from which readers read them is also a vital factor in the hermeneutic richness of the global church'.[76] In other words, we are living in a time when we have an extraordinary opportunity to enjoy a richness of understanding because of the global nature of the church. Wright continues: 'What persons of one culture bring from that culture to the reading of a text may illuminate dimensions or implications of the text itself that persons of another culture may not have read so clearly.'[77] Through our contexts, each of us has the opportunity for a fresh reading of Scripture that is helpful to our context and other parts of the global church. What an invitation!

---

[67] Wright, 55.

[68] Wright, 55.

[69] Tim J. Davy, *The Book of Job and the Mission of God: A Missional Reading* (Eugene: Pickwick Publications, 2020), 98.

[70] Davy, 131.

[71] Davy, 215.

[72] Davy, 215.

[73] Davy, 215.

[74] Davy, 168.

[75] Davy, 193.

[76] Wright, 39.

[77] Wright, 39.

The Role of the Triune God in Mission

We now shift from reading a Bible book through a missional hermeneutic to consider the theological topic of the intentions and functions of the triune missionary God as the source of mission. Attempting to explain the Trinitarian basis of mission is complex, depending on whether one approaches this from a doctrinal understanding of the Trinity or explores it functionally only. We choose the latter because to thoroughly investigate the oneness of the triune God or the distinctive roles within the Godhead and how this serves mission is beyond the scope of this work.

All the Trinity

Mission involves all members of the triune God. For example, 'a formulaic articulation of the *missio Dei*' has been: 'the Father sends the Son, the Son sends the Spirit, and Father and Son send the church in the power of the Spirit'.[78] Another way is to state that the Father proclaims the kingdom, the Son offers new life, and the Holy Spirit bears witness to the activity of the triune God. Lalsangkima Pachuau describes it this way: 'We focus our attention on the incarnation of Christ, as the channel of God's mission in the power of the Holy Spirit.'[79] Only through the triune God does the church have 'missional authority' to proclaim and demonstrate the gospel.[80]

The issue of authority is significant. Under Christendom's influence, biblical Trinitarian authority for mission was 'replaced by a cultural, institutional, or pragmatic one'.[81] With Christendom's diminishing influence, such authority is now 'utterly discredited'.[82] This lies behind the call for a Trinitarian missiology; a call to return to the authority of the triune God in mission.

The Scriptures reveal specific roles: the Father as creator and king possessing a kingdom. The Son who comes to offer new life and to bear the world's pain and brokenness that we might be restored. The Spirit 'is the primary actor' in mission[83] and brings life and power so that the people of God can participate with and witness to the triune God. Amos Yong draws upon patristic church father Irenaeus's metaphor of 'the two hands of the Father' – God's purposes are achieved through his two hands – Christ the Word, and the Holy Spirit: 'God works all things with the divine hands: by and through *both* Word and Spirit.'[84]

---

[78] Michael Goheen, *The Church and its Vocation: Lesslie Newbigin's Missionary Ecclessiology* (Grand Rapids: Baker Academic, 2018), 70.

[79] Lalsangkima Pachuau, *God at Work in the World: Theology and Mission in the Global Church* (Grand Rapids: Baker Academic, 2022), 17.

[80] Tennent, 67.

[81] Tennent, 67.

[82] Tennent, 67.

[83] Goheen, *The Church and its Vocation: Lesslie Newbigin's Missionary Ecclessiology*, 70.

[84] Amos Yong, *Beyond the Impasse: Toward a Pneumatological Theology of Religions* (Grand Rapids: Baker Academic, 2003), 43.

Throughout the Scriptures, we encounter an unfolding understanding of the roles within the Trinity. Theologians refer to *perichoresis*, the mutual indwelling relationship of the members of the triune God, Father, Son, and Spirit, who only exist through mutuality, the working and weaving together of who they are. It is the same with their roles. They cannot be separated neatly because they engage in them together.

The glorification of the triune God in mission occurs as 'the Father sent the Son to accomplish this redemption, so he sends the Spirit to apply this redemption to the hearts of men and women'.[85] God enables the church in his mission for witness and service. The redemptive movement originates from the triune God, flows through the church into the world, and 'results in people of every tribe, tongue, and nation responding in lifelong worship of God'.[86] The climax of the *missio Dei* occurs when 'God creates a new heaven and new earth'.[87]

Perhaps surprisingly, within the Protestant mission movement, the centrality of the triune God in mission is a relatively new focus. For much of the Protestant missionary era, mission has not been viewed primarily as the mission of God but as the church's work.

Surveying the Trinity

Interpreting mission through the Trinity takes various forms. There are three common views. First, the *immanent* Trinity is the eternal 'being of God as he is in himself' and as he 'seeks to draw humanity into his eternal glory'.[88] This is 'Christology "from above"' with the missional outcome that 'the promise of eternal life [which] concentrates on bringing people into a personal relationship with God'.[89] In this regard, the Trinity functions with 'the Father's work' presenting 'the kingdom as the climax of history. In Jesus and by the work of the Spirit, that kingdom is now present.'[90] However, this view can appear distant to 'the suffering and injustices of the world'.[91]

Second, the *economic* Trinity focuses on the history of salvation of the triune God carrying out the *missio Dei* 'through his engagement with the world'.[92] Lesslie Newbigin saw the 'work and mission of God narrated in the biblical story [as] fundamentally historical'.[93] This view 'from below' is a 'spirituality [that]

---

[85] Stetzer, and Nation, 8.

[86] Stetzer, and Nation, 8.

[87] Stetzer, and Nation, 8.

[88] John Corrie, *Dictionary of Mission Theology: Evangelical Foundations*, ed. John Corrie (Downers Grove: IVP Academic, 2007), 397.

[89] Corrie, 397.

[90] Goheen, *The Church and its Vocation: Lesslie Newbigin's Missionary Ecclessiology*, 70.

[91] Corrie, 397.

[92] Corrie, 397.

[93] Goheen, *The Church and its Vocation: Lesslie Newbigin's Missionary Ecclessiology*, 70.

is world-affirming'.[94] Mission 'concentrates on historical/cultural engagement and personal/social transformation'.[95] This view, however, can lose hold of 'transcendence and the "hope of glory"'.[96]

Third, the *social* Trinity describes the love between the three persons in 'a committed community. It also sees love as intrinsic to the nature of God.'[97] 'The gospel offers us a share in the divine *koinonia*, which leads into the love of God and fellowship with one another 'so that, as the church, we experience the "unity of diversity" of the Trinitarian relationships. The goal of mission becomes the creation of a community in which there is freedom for one another and fellowship with one another in commitment to one another.'[98] Social Trinitarianism, however, 'can lose touch with a personal God' because the view presents an 'irresistible social dimension of mission' that wants humanity to 'reflect the perfect community of the Trinity'.[99]

Pachuau calls social Trinitarianism 'one of the most creative and productive interpretations' that can serve as a model for partnering in mission.[100] Kenneth Shreve elaborates how the triune God sets the example for this:

> The distinct roles within the Trinity [demonstrate] that diversity within unity makes for a rich community. This is a good example for those involved in partnerships, as they learn to honor different roles and those who represent them. There does not need to be competition. When each role flows in the power of God, the unified whole becomes a blessing.[101]

Table 6 gives a matrix of how the three views of the triune God in mission can be viewed.

Views of Trinity	Characteristics	Weakness
Immanent	Eternal being of God; he seeks to draw humanity into his eternal glory; promise of eternal life; bringing people into a personal relationship with God; from above	Can be distant to the suffering and injustices of the world
Economic	History of salvation of the triune God through his engagement with the world; spirituality that is world-affirming; historical/cultural engagement	Can lose hold of transcendence and the hope of glory

---

[94] Corrie, 397.

[95] Corrie, 397.

[96] Corrie, 397.

[97] Corrie, 397.

[98] Corrie, 397.

[99] Corrie, 397.

[100] Pachuau, *God at Work in the World: Theology and Mission in the Global Church*, 24.

[101] Kenneth Shreve, *Partnership Theology in Creative Access Regions* (Carlisle: Langham Global Library, 2017), 71.

	and personal/social transformation; from below	
Social	Love as intrinsic to the nature of God; share in the divine *koinonia*; unity of diversity; creation of a community of freedom for one another and fellowship with one another	Can lose touch with a personal God because of a social dimension of mission that wants to reflect the perfect community of the Trinity

Table 6: Matrix of the Trinity in Mission

God's Cooperative Action

Let's consider the cooperative action of the triune God. For example, Jesus tells his followers about the arrival of 'the Holy Spirit, whom the Father will send in my name' (John 14:26, NIV). Here, all three members of the triune God are mentioned. Newbigin summarises the triune God's function in mission 'as proclaiming the kingdom of the Father, as sharing the life of the Son, and as bearing the witness of the Spirit'.[102] Mission in this 'trinitarian model' involves the Father holding all things together 'in his hand' through his divine care.[103] In the incarnation of Jesus, 'God was pleased to have all his fullness dwell in the Son' (Col. 1:19, NET). God's redemptive plan continues 'through the presence and active working of the Holy Spirit who is the presence [and preview] of the reign of God'.[104] Kenneth Shreve states that 'the Persons of the Godhead are intricately involved together in achieving the end result [of] redemption and salvation'.[105] Shreve notes that this interrelationship 'is displayed in the salvation story, where the Father sends the Son. The Spirit fills and guides the Son. The Son embraces the cross and, through his death and resurrection, enables the reconciliation between God and man.'[106] We see God's agency working out in his (1) divine action with humans, (2) collaboration with people, and (3) focus on salvation. Let's explore each of these.

Presence and Intention

In his grace, God offers a divine call to participate and collaborate in his mission. Allen Yeh observes, 'It is God who initiates, and we are merely partners in the endeavor.'[107] This echoes Jesus' invitation: 'Just as the Father has sent me, I also send you' (John 20:21, NET). There is a mystery here: God does not need human

---

[102] Newbigin, 29.

[103] Lesslie Newbigin, *The Gospel in a Pluralist Society* (Grand Rapids: Wm B. Eerdmans, 1989), 118.

[104] Newbigin, 118.

[105] Shreve, 72.

[106] Shreve, 72.

[107] Yeh, 20.

instrumentality but 'chooses the risky course of partnership'.[108] God's actions are risky by human standards, starting with appointing the first disciples. They were Zealots, Roman sympathisers, Galileans, and Essenes who held very different social and theological positions. Jesus' disciples, as his co-workers in a collaborative ministry, are entrusted with a global mission (Matt. 28:18-20). The Apostle Paul continues expressing this collaborative nature of mission through creating shared ministry networks among co-workers such as Aquila and Priscilla (1 Cor. 16:19), itinerant preachers such as Barnabas (Acts 13:2) and Silas (Acts 15:40), young recruits like Timothy (Acts 16:3), and many more (Rom. 16:21-24).

Turning to partnership in mission, Cathy Ross states that 'partnership is an idea essential to the very nature of God', and she doesn't 'think it is pushing the idea too far to say that we see partnership in the Godhead. God is a community... of three divine persons; God is also one God. These realities allow... for relationship [and] unity and diversity.'[109] Enoch Wan and Kevin Penman note how 'the Godhead (its relationship, love, and unity–diversity) [is] seen as the starting point for understanding partnership'.[110] Shreve observes that 'diversity is not something to disparage but to embrace [because it] embraces the creative genius of the Almighty God. God has determined that each part should have its own function.'[111] The triune God 'is characterized by love. This divine love is found in the reciprocal interdependence and the dedication towards each other of the Trinitarian members. Indeed, there is no God other than the Father, Son, and Spirit bound together in the active relations of love throughout eternity.'[112]

This immediately gives us a clue about how we engage in God's mission. God's character is missional, and creation is a missional act, the movement of the triune God extending the divine community of love beyond God's self to the whole created order. In the introductory chapters of Genesis, this missional God invites Adam and Eve, those made in his image, to participate in his mission, telling them to be fruitful, to fill the earth, to take mastery of it, to subdue it. The triune God not only creates out of missional love but then immediately invites these creatures to participate in his mission. All this occurred before the Fall.

Collaboration with People

Kenneth Shreve sets this foundation of collaborating:

> The triune God exists in a relationship of love and unity. God, in his sovereignty and wisdom, created the world and mankind to rule it... God's desire is to see the broken relationship [with humankind because of the fall] restored, and all things

---

[108] Balia, and Kim, 129.

[109] Cathy Ross, "The Theology of Partnership," *International Bulletin of Missionary Research* 34, no. 3 (2010): 146.

[110] Enoch Wan, and Kevin Penman, "The 'Why,' 'How' and 'Who' of Partnership in Christian Missions," *Global Missiology* (April 2010): 3.

[111] Shreve, 98.

[112] John R. Franke, in *Reading the Bible Missionally*, ed. Michael Goheen (Grand Rapids: Wm B. Eerdmans, 2016, Kindle edition), 1987.

brought together under the headship of his Son…. This plan includes partnership with humankind, whom he created in his image.[113]

Throughout the Old Testament, God reveals his plan, including how he 'chose to work with Abraham, who was called his friend. The plan grew to a partnership with a nation, whom he called to be his chosen people.'[114] The pattern continues to the coming of the Messiah in the New Testament. Cathy Ross observes, 'In the incarnation, God communicates himself to us and establishes a relationship with us.'[115] It is through the incarnation of the Son of God that the triune God informs partnering with him. Shreve continues: 'After the death and resurrection of Jesus, the partnership rose to a whole new level, as the Father and the Son sent the Holy Spirit to indwell and to lead the church.'[116]

At the Willingen International Missionary Conference in 1952, the Trinitarian mission was understood as 'the love of the Father who sent his Son to reconcile all things to himself. The Son sent the Spirit to gather his church together and empower it to participate in his mission.'[117] Jesus sends his church 'to continue his mission, and this sending defines its very nature'.[118] Therefore, 'God is now partnering with the worldwide body of Christ', his church sent by Jesus, the instruments to continue his mission.[119] This sending defines its very nature. In a partnership framework, God is 'involved with us in a supreme act of trust', he's 'responsible for our redemption', and his 'self-emptying, supremely upon the cross, was the liability accepted by God for our creation and was God's freely chosen means for our redemption'.[120]

Since God is mission by nature, the church is to be engaged in God's mission. German theologian Karl Hartenstein described mission as an 'attribute of God',[121] who acts as a 'fountain of sending love' because of God's love for people.[122] However, as Shreve states, 'partnership must be focused on wherever and with whomever the Holy Spirit determines; and that may or may not be the local congregation'.[123] Yet the New Testament, especially through the Apostle Paul's letters, discusses a range of foundations, relationships, and implications for the body of Christ acting in partnership with God in his mission. Shreve notes how the foundation for mission partnership is the body of Christ: 'It proclaims that everyone is on the same team and that God has determined individuals' roles. Jesus is the head, and the Holy Spirit is in control. Right relationship with God and with fellow believers is the expected standard of operation.'[124]

---

[113] Shreve, 91.

[114] Shreve, 92.

[115] Ross, 147.

[116] Shreve, 92.

[117] Goheen, 240.

[118] Goheen, 240.

[119] Shreve, 92.

[120] Ross, 147.

[121] Oborji, *Concepts of Mission: The Evolution of Contemporary Missiology*, 134.

[122] Bosch, *Transforming Mission: Paradigm Shifts in Theology of Mission*, 402.

[123] Shreve, 32.

[124] Shreve, 117.

Focus on Salvation

The prominent teaching of Jesus was the announcement of the kingdom of God's arrival through his miracles and bold teaching. The kingdom, or reign of God, 'represents the dynamic activity of God and the sphere in which his rule is experienced.'[125] Arthur Glasser helps us understand the triune God's role in his kingdom, now and not yet:

> Jesus Christ is indeed the fulfillment of Scripture. Salvation is only available through faith in him. Indeed, apart from him, there is no salvation. And the time is now to proclaim this message to the nations. The coming of the Holy Spirit at Pentecost gave birth to the church, mobilizing and empowering the church to be God's primary instrument for announcing the kingdom of God among the nations of the earth.[126]

The loving God invites all people into the presence of his kingdom through new life in Christ. People who become part of God's community follow the Holy Spirit wherever and whenever he leads them. God gives the church its role as he initiates mission and empowers and dispatches the church as his primary instrument – a sent community.

God's agency in mission is intentional. He acts out of love and collaborates with the people of God as his instrument. This holistic approach encompasses proclaiming the gospel, discipling followers of Christ, demonstrating the gospel (including transforming all that is unjust), and stewarding God's creation.

The triune God's agency, with the scope and focus of his plan of redemption and reconciliation of all that was lost in the Fall, is shown in Table 7.

Presence and intention of the triune God	Collaboration between the triune God and people	Focus on salvation
God is the initiator of his mission	God desires to see the broken relationship restored and all things brought together under the headship of Jesus	The prominent teaching of Jesus is the announcement of the kingdom of God
God gives us a divine call to participate in his mission (John 20:21)	God's pattern of partnership with humankind	The dynamic activity of God where his rule is experienced
There's a mystery in God's use of a human instrumentality	In the Incarnation God communicates himself and establishes relationship	Salvation is only through faith in Christ
God's missional actions are risky by human standards	Father and Son send the Holy Spirit to indwell and to lead the church	The Holy Spirit empowers the church to be God's primary instrument for

---

[125] Arthur Glasser, *Announcing the Kingdom* (Grand Rapids: Baker Academic, 2003), 226.
[126] Glasser, 325.

Presence and intention of the triune God	Collaboration between the triune God and people	Focus on salvation
		announcing the kingdom of God to the nations
God is a community of three divine persons; God is also one God	The Son sends the Spirit to gather and empower the church to participate in his mission	The triune God invites all people into the presence of his kingdom through new life in Christ
The triune community allows for relationship and unity and diversity	Jesus sends his church to continue his mission	The triune God gives the church its role in mission
Divine love is found in reciprocal interdependence of the triune God	Mission is an attribute of God and his sending love	The church is God's primary instrument as a sent community
God extends the divine community of love to the whole created order as a missional act	The body of Christ acts in partnership with God in his mission	A holistic approach of proclaiming the gospel, discipling followers, demonstrating the gospel, and stewarding creation

Table 7: God's Agency in Mission Theology

The Triune God and the Church

What is the role of the church in God's mission? Rather than mission originating from the church or being church-centred, the triune God initiates mission and empowers the church to reach out to the world as witness-bearers. However, the church's role is not marginalised to mission, even though God's mission is more than the missionary actions of the church itself. The church's role is to be 'an instrument of mission… in the movement of God's love' for all humanity.[127]

Significantly, God empowers not only individuals but the whole church for mission. The Scriptures demonstrate that what we encounter in the New Testament is not God introducing a new tactic or a different way of working. Looking at all of Scripture, we see consistency in God's approach. He has always called out people to participate in his life and be his witness-bearers. This is the Old Testament account of Israel's primary calling to live as the gathered people of God under his rule, thus demonstrating who God is in contrast to the surrounding nations and, as a result, bearing witness and serving as a light to the nations. Because of the frailty of the old covenant, this went unfulfilled, yet we see in the New Testament the continuation of the people of God as central in the way that God carries out his mission.

---

[127] Oborji, *Concepts of Mission: The Evolution of Contemporary Missiology*, 135.

The church's understanding of mission should begin with the triune God, continue from there, and from there, find its completion. The church 'acts out the love of Jesus that took him to the cross' when it invites people into a union with Jesus Christ, who in this world is 'the presence of the kingdom'. As the 'preview' of God's kingdom, the Holy Spirit directs the church into the world, often in mysterious ways.[128]

Only through this triune God of mission does the church have any missional authority to proclaim and demonstrate the gospel. The triune God gives the church its role in his mission. This is 'the whole church taking the whole gospel to the whole person in the whole world'.[129] The triune God has drawn the church into his community and made the church a genuine participant in his mission. This is a staggering responsibility and privilege. The scope of God's mission is to 'restore all nations [and] all cultures from the sinful rebellion of humankind and its effects'.[130]

Recognising the recent and current era of Christendom – particularly the Protestant mission movement – we acknowledge that the influence of a Trinitarian authorisation for mission was weakened under Christendom, sometimes replaced by a cultural, institutional, or pragmatic authority. Specifically, there is a sense that as cultures from the West grew and developed, mission came to be as much about civilising as about bringing the gospel. It seems that now the Christendom model of mission has become unhelpful and even obstructive. With Christendom's waning influence, this basis of authority for mission is markedly discredited, leading many to consider the term 'mission' off-putting, rejecting the idea that the church has a right to engage in mission. And yet, this right, this authority, to engage in mission comes not from the church but from God, who is himself missional.

The Triune God and Community

Since the triune God is the perfect embodiment of hope and the originator and source of mission, he calls and enables his people to be a community of hope while behaving as a contrast community that engages with, while not conforming to, all that surrounds it.

The relationality of this aspect becomes very important. Unfortunately, we have often seen the relational aspect of mission in quite individualistic terms. The Scriptures, however, see mission primarily in communal terms. Since the triune God is a perfect embodiment of hope and the source of mission, he calls and enables his people to be a community of hope that reflects him. This community speaks of the depth of the relationship, a relationship which Jesus describes extraordinarily as having the same dimension as the relationship of Father, Son, and Spirit. In John 17, Jesus prays for his disciples that they would be one as he, the Spirit, and the Father were one. This relationship of love is the

---

[128] Newbigin, 65.

[129] Goheen, *Introducing Christian Mission Today: Scripture, History and Issues*, 26.

[130] Goheen, *Introducing Christian Mission Today: Scripture, History and Issues*, 39.

most powerful witness to the watching world that Jesus Christ truly is Lord. In a world of fragmentation, in a world of selfishness and greed, in a world of broken identity, the witness of the people of God across the nations is designed to make a statement that Jesus Christ is able to bring everyone and everything under his Lordship.

This friendship relationship within the triune God sets the example of divine and human friendship through God's invitation to participate in his relational life. He calls us to friendship, first with himself, then with others. An intimate relationship formed with the triune God in community and friendship with others represents the most basic foundation for mission.

The Triune God in the Great Commission

A shift towards a Trinitarian understanding of theological foundations for mission portrays all three members of the triune God as actively participating in the *missio Dei*. Although we are focusing here on the Trinitarian nature of Jesus' final recorded instructions to his disciples, our understanding of the Trinitarian nature of God's mission is drawn from the whole testimony of Scripture and not simply these texts. Nonetheless, it is worth considering the Trinitarian link in these texts. In doing so, we offer the observation from Christopher Wright that the Great Commission 'is not referred to as an explicit driver for the missionary expansion of the church in the New Testament after Acts 1'.[131]

William Carey (1761–1834) is called the father of the modern missionary movement. In his booklet *Enquiry into the Obligation of Christians to Use Means for the Conversion of Heathens* (1792), Carey wanted to determine whether 'the commission given by our Lord to His disciples [is] still binding on us'.[132] He was referring to Matthew 28:18-20, which became famously known as the Great Commission. Carey himself used the term commission, never Great Commission. (The date of when this text was given the heading 'The Great Commission' in our Bibles was sometime between 1600 and 1800 AD). The Matthew 28:18-20 (NLT) text reads:

> I have been given all authority in heaven and on earth. [19] Therefore, go and make disciples of all the nations [or all peoples], baptizing them in the name of the Father and the Son and the Holy Spirit. [20] Teach these new disciples to obey all the commands I have given you. And be sure of this: I am with you always, even to the end of the age.

This text is Trinitarian because the baptising of new disciples into God's community is in the name of all three members of the triune God – the Father, the Son, and the Holy Spirit. The triune God gives 'a call to a personal relationship with Jesus, who has ushered in his kingdom'. The triune God 'demands radical loyalty and commitment' and an invitation 'into a community

---

[131] Wright, 36.
[132] Robert Hunt, *The Gospel Among the Nations: A Documentary History of Inculturation* (Maryknoll: Orbis Books, 2010), 83.

chosen to participate in God's mission to the world'. This is a 'summons' to people into 'a lifestyle of obedience that is costly and comprehensive'.[133]

Four other Bible texts record similar last words from Jesus to his disciples. The others are in chronological order starting with John 20:19-23 (NLT):

> That Sunday evening, the disciples were meeting behind locked doors because they were afraid of the Jewish leaders. Suddenly, Jesus was standing there among them! 'Peace be with you,' he said. [20] As he spoke, he showed them the wounds in his hands and his side. They were filled with joy when they saw the Lord! [21] Again he said, 'Peace be with you. As the Father has sent me, so I am sending you.' [22] Then he breathed on them and said, 'Receive the Holy Spirit. [23] If you forgive anyone's sins, they are forgiven. If you do not forgive them, they are not forgiven.'

This passage has an obvious Trinitarian perspective because all three members of the triune God are mentioned: The Father is the sender ('As the Father has sent me…'). Jesus appears as the sent one and sends the disciples. The Holy Spirit is revealed to the disciples ('Receive….') and gives his presence, guidance, and empowerment of the mission. 'Mission can only be carried out in the power of the Spirit as the church shares in the resurrection life of Christ.'[134] Sung Chan Kwon notes that 'the foundation for sending is the relationship and oneness between the Father and the Son and knowing the will of the Father in the relationship'.[135] As the disciples go, a new community of transformed disciples is formed, resulting in gathered believers – the church.

The cross of Jesus is the distinction of our Christian faith. The scars of our risen Lord prove his identity. In response, Jesus wants us to be obedient to his mission. It's an assignment of self-emptying and humble service, even in precarious times and difficult situations. When the disciples saw Jesus' wounds, they must have realised that obedience to God's mission involves suffering and inconvenience. However, in addition, Jesus immediately gave them the promise of the Holy Spirit. While humans are involved in planning and action, it is primarily not about us, our activity, or our initiative. Instead, it is God's invitation to his people to participate in his mission. We now look at the second passage of Luke 24:36-49 (NLT), when Jesus suddenly appears among his disciples:

> Then he said, 'When I was with you before, I told you that everything written about me in the law of Moses and the prophets and in the Psalms must be fulfilled.' [45] Then he opened their minds to understand the Scriptures. [46] And he said, 'Yes, it was written long ago that the Messiah would suffer and die and rise from the dead on the third day. [47] It was also written that this message would be proclaimed in the authority of his name to all the nations, beginning in Jerusalem: "There is forgiveness of sins for all who repent." [48] You are witnesses of all these things. [49] And now I will send the Holy Spirit, just as my Father promised. But stay here in the city until the Holy Spirit comes and fills you with power from heaven.'

---

[133] Goheen, *The Church and its Vocation: Lesslie Newbigin's Missionary Ecclessiology*, 96.

[134] Goheen, *The Church and its Vocation: Lesslie Newbigin's Missionary Ecclessiology*, 128.

[135] Kwon, 179.

This passage has an obvious Trinitarian perspective because Jesus reveals himself to the disciples; they are his witnesses. He tells them he is sending them the Holy Spirit, just as the Father promised, indicating the interrelationship of the triune God's involvement in these plans and purpose. For us today, 'the church continues Jesus' ministry of deliverance from the power of sin' ('There is forgiveness of sins for all who repent').[136] Now, the next passage of Mark 16:14-18 (NLT):

> Jesus appeared as the disciples were eating together... [15] And then he told them, 'Go into all the world and preach the Good News to everyone. [16] Anyone who believes and is baptized will be saved. But anyone who refuses to believe will be condemned. [17] These miraculous signs will accompany those who believe: they will cast out demons in my name, and they will speak in new languages. [18] They will be able to handle snakes with safety, and if they drink anything poisonous, it won't hurt them. They will be able to place their hands on the sick, and they will be healed.' [19] When the Lord Jesus had finished talking with them, he was taken up into heaven and sat down in the place of honor at God's right hand. [20] And the disciples went everywhere and preached, and the Lord worked through them, confirming what they said by many miraculous signs.

The Trinitarian perspective from this passage is this: Jesus will take his place of authority beside the Father. Signs will be given to confirm the Word and demonstrate the presence of the Lord. Although not mentioned explicitly, Word and sign demonstrate the Spirit's power, as this is no purely human agency at work. Mark is typically succinct in his rendering of the final words of Jesus. But this text cannot be separated from two verses 19–20, as is commonly done, which record the ascension and Jesus taking his place of authority beside the Father. In addition, signs are given as confirmation of the Word and demonstrate the presence of the Lord. And now, this final text of Acts 1:6-8 (NLT):

> So when the apostles were with Jesus, they kept asking him, 'Lord, has the time come for you to free Israel and restore our kingdom?'" [7] He replied, 'The Father alone has the authority to set those dates and times, and they are not for you to know. [8] But you will receive power when the Holy Spirit comes upon you. And you will be my witnesses, telling people about me everywhere – in Jerusalem, throughout Judea, in Samaria, and to the ends of the earth.'

The entire book of Acts is often considered the 'Acts of the Holy Spirit' rather than the 'Acts of the Apostles'. This text is also Trinitarian: Jesus is present ('when the apostles were with Jesus, they kept asking him...') Jesus references that only God the Father 'has the authority to set those dates and times'. Jesus concludes with 'You will receive power when the Holy Spirit comes upon you.' The Spirit will form the disciples as witnesses as they 'enter new places to become new people by joining themselves to those in Judea, Samaria, and the ends of the earth'.[137] 'The ends of the earth is the ultimate horizon of God's

---

[136] Goheen, *The Church and its Vocation: Lesslie Newbigin's Missionary Ecclessiology*, 128.
[137] Jennings, 18.

mission.'[138] We also see how 'geography matters. Place matters to God. From a specific place, the disciples will move forward into the world. To go from place to place is to go from people to people and to go from an old identity to a new one.'[139]

These five passages from the four gospels and Acts can be taken together as the Great Commission from our Lord to make him known and make disciples of the nations. These texts, expressly thought to be central to understanding God's mission, show how the triune God is specifically mentioned in each of them. Table 8 summarises the Trinitarian dimension of them.

Text	Trinitarian Mention
Matthew 28:18-20	Baptising of new disciples is to be done in the name of all three members
John 20:19-23	The Father is the sender, Jesus is the sent one, the Holy Spirit is revealed for his presence, guidance, and empowerment
Luke 24:26-48	Jesus mentions the sending of the Holy Spirit just as the Father promised
Mark 16:14-18	Jesus takes his place beside the Father; signs confirm the Word and demonstrate the presence of the Lord; Word and sign demonstrate the Spirit's power
Acts 1:6-8	The apostles were with Jesus, he references God the Father, he promises the Holy Spirit

Table 8: The Triune God in the Great Commission Texts

Summary

We looked at components and examples of missional hermeneutics. We explored how missiologists read the Book of Job, the Gospel of John, and the epistles of Colossians and Ephesians. Their work helps us ensure we are not proof-texting the Scriptures – finding a Bible passage supporting our missional perspective. Instead, we are encouraged to read the Bible through a missional hermeneutic matrix.

Finally, we considered how mission originates from the heart of the triune missionary God – the source for Mission Theology. Mission is planned by the Father, who proclaims the kingdom; embodied in the Son, who offers new life; and empowered by the Holy Spirit, who bears witness to the activity of the whole of the triune God. Reflecting the nature of the relationship of the triune God, God's people are called from and into their contexts and situations to bring the whole gospel to the whole world.

---

[138] Goheen, *The Church and its Vocation: Lesslie Newbigin's Missionary Ecclessiology*, 99.
[139] Jennings, 16.

Let us consider what we have discovered so far:

• Mission originates from God.

• The goal of mission is *shalom*: the redemption and renewal of the whole creation, where the prayer of Jesus is fulfilled, 'Your kingdom come, your will be done.' In other words, it is the reign of God fully restored, in which all things in heaven and earth find their place together under the Lordship of Jesus.

• Mission Theology is derived from the narrative of the whole Scripture.

• Mission involves the whole church, since the entire church is called to bear witness to God's purposes and activities, fulfilled in Jesus Christ.

• Wherever mission structures exist, they should facilitate the work of the whole church in mission and not operate separately from it.

• Our posture within God's mission includes wonder, worship, dependence, prayer, humility, and celebration.

Reflective Questions:

• How could you apply the criteria from the Comparison of Missional Hermeneutics (Table 5) to do a missional reading of any passage of the Bible?
• How do these observations of the triune God's activity in the Great Commission texts inform your involvement in and practice of mission?

7. How We Describe Mission Matters

Introduction

In this chapter, we consider definitions of mission and how they relate to Mission Theology. Looking carefully at terminology is important. It may go without saying, but language matters! Language is not simply a vehicle for expressing what we believe. It creates, shapes, establishes, and reinforces what we believe. In a media-intense world, slogans are powerful. In missions, we also implement slogans to communicate. Think about some of the slogans we use, what they mean, the power they exert, and the emotions they evoke. Some slogans about mission include: 'The 10/40 Window', 'Unengaged, Unreached People Groups' (UUPGs), 'Bibleless Peoples', or 'Church Planting Movements', and 'Finish the Task'.

Consider three of these: (1) With UUPGs, we are encouraged to adopt a group because they are currently unreached. If we do this, they will be reached. We are key because what we do becomes the most important element in the gospel coming to this otherwise lost group. (2) With Finish the Task, the emphasis is on speed, scale, and strategy. This gives the idea that mission is essentially a task to be performed. There is something finite that we can complete. (3) With Church Planting Movements, problems arise when church planting gets primacy over other disciple-making expressions of the Lordship of Christ. These three examples show how mission which is meant to be 'relational in its nature in being derived from the God of love, becomes transactional'.[1] These slogans reduce the complexities in mission to a simplistic and formulaic approach to mission.

The Invitation to Come

Biblical texts such as the Great Commission of Matthew 28:18-20 help us understand the triune God in mission. Through this one passage more than any other part of Scripture, much of the Protestant cross-cultural mission movement of the past two hundred years has inspired, motivated, and shaped the church's comprehension of mission. For most generations since Carey, the primary command driving mission has been 'Go'. This is understandable given the strong biblical support for the importance of 'going' in mission.

In contrast, we can pursue biblical texts that can help us respond appropriately to the current context for mission, not just the Great Commission texts. For

---

[1] Paul Bendor-Samuel, "Challenge and Realignment in the Protestant Cross-Cultural Mission Movement," *Transformation* 34, no. 4 (2017): 272.

example, in the book of Acts, we see the church engaging in God's mission more broadly than the narrow ways we've adopted. In Acts 8:2, we observe the whole church scattered from Jerusalem throughout the regions of Judea and Samaria because of persecution – all except the apostles, who remained in Jerusalem. Often, Christians had to move out, not because they were sent, but for their own safety.

The only Christians equipped to remain in place in the missionary role were the apostles. In Acts 13, we witness the commissioning and sending out of Paul, Saul, and Barnabas, whom the Holy Spirit, speaking to the church leaders in Antioch, sets apart for the work of mission. Instead of the command to go out, we see a different paradigm, which is the invitation to 'come' join what God is already doing – 'Come over to Macedonia and help us' (Acts 16:9). The invitation in the vision is made by God. Paul sees a man of Macedonia inviting him. But when he gets to Macedonia, he does not meet a man but a woman, Lydia. His vision was none other than the Lord inviting Paul to come and join him in the work he was already doing. Appearing as a man of Macedonia, the Lord identifies himself with those he is calling Paul to work among. God was telling Paul, 'I am at work here and I invite you to join me!'

The invitation to come is an essential counterpoint to the command to go. The invitation to come is, first, an invitation to discipleship. Like the command to go, it too can be traced through Scripture. For example, in Matthew 4:18-19, Jesus tells Simon, Peter and Andrew to 'Come, follow me… and I will make you fishers of men.' 'Come' is the starting point. Before Jesus sends his disciples into mission, they are first invited to come join him. A missional hermeneutic involves much more than the Great Commission texts.

The Terminology of Mission

We have considered the technical language of mission, starting with *missio Dei*, the mission of God. By delving into this topic, we carefully examine other related terms, endeavouring to understand and use mission language more accurately, and to better inform our Mission Theology, reflection, and practice.

Michael Stroope gives us a comprehensive basis for examining how the 'language of mission' is used, stating that it 'is important because our talk about mission determines who we are and what we do. Language forms identity as words shape and express belief and ideals, choices and purpose.'[2] Not only that, there is widespread confusion and misuse – and therefore misunderstanding – of mission terminology within the community of practitioners and theorists of mission. We have reached the point where 'almost anybody using the concept of mission has to explain how it is understood if serious confusion is to be avoided'.[3]

Although the term mission might seem uncomplicated and easy to understand, it carries all kinds of baggage. Though present everywhere, it remains

---

[2] Stroope, xiii.
[3] Stroope, xiii.

mysterious, despite being – according to Stroope – 'a rather common word with seemingly obvious and straightforward meaning. Yet, on closer inspection, the meaning of mission is not so ordinary or straightforward. In its many specialized and technical uses, mission is complex and often bewildering.'[4]

Stroope clarifies the use of 'mission as a lexeme, a lexical unit of meaning' and other forms and variants such as missions, *missio*, missionary, and missional 'are… little more than derivatives of the singular form'.[5] That is the linguistic aspect of it. But there is also the question of whether it is biblical. If it is, 'what does it mean? If not, when did the church begin using mission language, and why? And what baggage might mission bring into its Christian use from those extrabiblical sources?'[6]

Definitions of Mission

Craig Ott offers insights that reflect numerous evangelical assumptions about mission over the past 200 years. He states that Christian mission is

> the overall purpose for which God sends the church into the world… The word 'mission' stems from the Latin term for 'sending.' God himself is a sending God, a missionary God, who sent prophets and angels as his messengers and who ultimately sent his Son as [the] agent of his redemptive purposes in the world. Today he sends the church in the power of the Spirit as his people to further his mission of redemption and restoration. The church is indeed God's missionary people, a sent people. As expressed in Jesus' words to his disciples, 'As the Father has sent me, even so I am sending you' (John 20:21).[7]

Evangelical Western missiologists define mission with general and specific dimensions in these examples:

- Michael Stroope: 'the effort, through various actions, to address the human condition, proselytize others, and spread the Christian faith'.[8] In this general sense, 'mission can refer to a variety of activities and emphases'.[9]
- Christopher Wright: 'Fundamentally, our mission (if it is biblically informed and validated) means our committed participation as God's people, at God's invitation and command, in God's own mission within the history of God's world for the redemption of God's creation.'[10]
- Robert Gallagher: 'the total undertaking God has assigned the church for the salvation of the world. The end result of mission is God, through the church and beyond, reaching across barriers of culture, language, geography,

---

[4] Stroope, 1.
[5] Stroope, xiii, fn 1.
[6] Stroope, 1.
[7] Ott, *The Church on Mission: A Biblical Vision for Transformation Among All People*, 2.
[8] Stroope, 5.
[9] Stroope, 5.
[10] Wright, 25.

ideology, and ethnicity to bring people to Christ by announcing the gospel in speech and social action.'[11]

• Mark Simon: 'Mission should not be limited to proclamation, but holistically encompass the just actions, character and witness of God's people crossing diverse geographic, ethnic, and economic boundaries in order to further God's redemptive plan for all creation.'[12]

• Michael Goheen and Jim Mullins: 'God's continuing work to restore creation and to our own active participation in that work.'[13]

• J.D. Payne's 'very simple definition of mission' is 'all that God has done, is doing, and will do to redeem sinful humans and recreate the cosmos into the new heavens and new earth'.[14]

For 'religious professionals, mission is seen as a specialty, or some would even say a science, with its own community of practitioners and scholars who use technical language and conduct specialized discussions... And yet, even among these specialists, the meaning of mission is varied and contested.'[15] Here are a few examples that illustrate some diversity in interpretation of the term:

• Mission for some 'is narrowly defined as "evangelism that results in churches," ... thus, mission emphasises proclamation to the near exclusion of other activities or emphases.'[16] (We are engaged in evangelism with the expectation that churches will be established.)

• The WCC's *Together Towards Life* states that evangelism is 'the communication of the whole gospel to the whole of humanity in the whole world'.[17] *Together Towards Life* defines mission as 'the church embodying God's salvation in this world'[18] when people are invited 'to become a part of the Christian community'.[19]

• *Ad Gentes* (6, 9) of the Roman Catholic Church: 'the activities through which the church does her mission – the work of evangelization and of planting the church itself among various cultures and peoples'.[20]

• Others use the term mission 'as the alternative or counterpoint to evangelism... mission is everything but evangelism [and] includes a long list

---

[11] Robert Gallagher, "Missionary Methods: St Paul's, St Rolland's, or Ours?" in *Missionary Methods: Research, Reflections, and Realities*, ed. Craig Ott and J.D. Payne (Pasadena: William Carey Library, 2013), 4.

[12] Simon, 39.

[13] Michael Goheen, and Jim Mullins, *The Symphony of Mission* (Grand Rapids: Baker Academic, 2019), 3.

[14] J.D. Payne, "Theology of Mission", *Strike the Match with J.D. Payne Podcast*, 22 November 2022, https://www.jdpayne.org/2022/11/theology-of-mission/?utm_source=rss&utm_medium=rss&utm_campaign=theology-of-mission.

[15] Stroope, 5.

[16] Stroope, 6.

[17] Keum, 29.

[18] Keum, 60.

[19] Keum, 63.

[20] Oborji, *Concepts of Mission: The Evolution of Contemporary Missiology*, 42.

of concerns and activities... Mission means anything and everything the church does, from discipleship to eldercare', etc.[21]

• It may exclude human involvement, even the church. 'Mission can include political and social action, peacemaking and reconciliation – even revolutionary activities and movements unrelated to the church or Christianity.'[22] Anything that can be conceived of as contributing to building God's kingdom – whether it's related to the church and Christianity or not – can become part of mission.

• Lalsangkima Pachuau: 'God's redemptive work or mission on behalf of his creation'.[23]

• John Stott stated that it included 'evangelism and social responsibility'.[24]

• Samuel Escobar said, 'mission must be holistic'.[25]

• Christopher Wright says it 'includes compassion toward and care for the whole of creation and a call to conversion, addressing both disease and planting churches'.[26]

• As a way of outlining 'the breadth of meaning in the word, and thus the extent of the problem', Stroope summarises definitions of mission as:

• '[a] general, common task of representation or personal assignment';

• '[a] specified aim or goal of a corporate entity';

• '[a] specified and personal life purpose or calling';

• 'evangelism and church planting';

• 'the ministry of the church in all of its forms';

• 'structures or entities related to the expansion of Christianity';

• 'the activity of God in the world, often with little to no reference to the church'.[27]

This overview demonstrates how mission has been defined – generally, specifically, and in all its usages. This is why Stroope notes that the term 'is prone to murkiness rather than clarity' and 'the jungle of mission verbiage stands badly in need of some cleaning up'.[28]

Mission and its Derivatives

In addition to seeking clarity on terminology definitions, there are terms related to mission to consider.

Missio Dei: Since we have already covered *missio Dei*, as a recap, Karl Barth and Karl Hartenstein's work with the term established it within ecumenical spheres in the 1930s–1950s. For the past 20 years, the term has been universally

---

[21] Stroope, 7.

[22] Stroope, 7.

[23] Pachuau, *God at Work in the World: Theology and Mission in the Global Church*, 1.

[24] Stroope, 8.

[25] Stroope, 8.

[26] Stroope, 8.

[27] Stroope, 10–11.

[28] Stroope, 12.

accepted and used, including by evangelicals. Stroope notes its wide use in this way: 'In most cases, proponents of *missio Dei* equate it with the singular form of mission, thereby aiming to distinguish the contemporary practice of mission from that of the triune God.'[29] 'For some, *missio Dei* refers to divine essence (this is who God is in himself), and for others, it signifies divine operation (this is what God does among humanity). Thus, one could say the who and what of God is *missio Dei*, and the who and what of the church is *missio ecclesia*.'

The *missio Dei* is an 'essential element of the divine character [and] attribute of God' because it is the salvation activity of the triune missionary God.[30] This means 'it will never come to a conclusion and must continue throughout eternity'.[31] Jesus Christ is proclaimed, through the blood of his cross, as universal saviour for all. By this means, God invites all people into the presence of his kingdom through new life in Christ. They become part of his community. God's will for his community – following the Holy Spirit wherever and whenever he leads – gives a preview of God's kingdom.

Mission 'is first and foremost about God and His redemptive purposes and initiatives in the world'.[32] Mission does not originate with or belong to the church, nor does it strictly concern itself with 'any actions or tasks or strategies or initiatives the church may undertake'.[33] The church's role in mission 'should be engaging the world, near and far, with the gospel'[34] because the triune God dispatches the church from where it is located as his primary instrument – a sent community to carry out his mission to be his witness across the world in a broad spectrum of ministry. Consequently, mission is not restricted to the activity of missionaries sent by the church, who go overseas and cross various barriers, to bring the message of salvation (with the caveat that in some spheres, this still describes mission).

The scope of mission is defined by the extent of God's mission – his Lordship overall. Consequently, 'All our mission must therefore reflect the integration of evangelism and committed engagement in the world.'[35] Through his integral or holistic mission, God is the good creator who makes all things new in his good but broken creation. God has purposed to bring reconciliation and transformation to the whole created order. We are called to join God in his purpose.

Missions: Generally, adding the 's' to 'mission' means 'the varied works and activities of the church to reflect and participate in God's mission'.[36] Simply, it refers to individual agencies involved in God's mission. These are the human instruments tasked with carrying out mission in God's world. In other words,

---

[29] Stroope, 16.

[30] John R. Franke, *Missional Theology: An Introduction* (Grand Rapids: Baker Academic, 2020), 8.

[31] Franke, *Missional Theology: An Introduction*, 8.

[32] Tennent, 54.

[33] Tennent, 54.

[34] Pachuau, *God at Work in the World: Theology and Mission in the Global Church*, 32.

[35] Rose Dowsett, *The Cape Town Commitment Study Edition* (Peabody: Hendrickson Publishers, 2012), 43.

[36] Pachuau, *God at Work in the World: Theology and Mission in the Global Church*, 1.

'Mission is divine activity, but missions includes human and ecclesial activity.'[37] Similarly, the 'capitalized Mission refers to divine activity, whereas lowercase mission is reserved for human endeavours'.[38]

Missional is an adjective describing something related to mission or something characterised by the mission of God, requiring that one be fully aligned with the mission of the triune God. The term is used to describe the relationships, purpose, and identity of churches and organisations and their leadership within the *missio Dei*. Stroope points out how missional 'has become the adjective of choice... [for example] missional church or missional endeavour', and then quotes Darrell Guder, saying that missional represents "'the merger of ecclesiology and missiology into one discipline."' Stroope quotes Darrell Guder, saying that missional represents "'the merger of ecclesiology and missiology into one discipline"'.[39] (One positive outcome emerging through this is that much of life and human activity and the church's activity has now been brought into an understanding of mission.)

These terms characterise activities and intent along a spectrum in the context of God's mission. These interrelationships are depicted in Diagram 7.

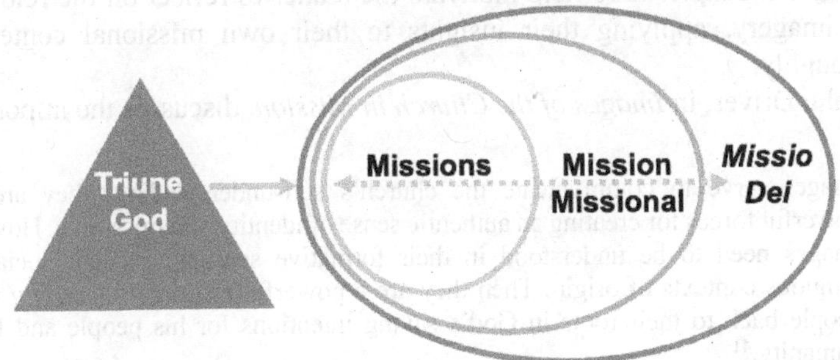

Diagram 7: Interrelationships of Terminology of God's Mission

Stroope notes that '*missional* is the adjective that describes anything associated with the *missio Dei*, and thus is the vehicle by which' some bring 'a host of concerns into the mission arena: *missional* people, *missional* theology, *missional* theologians... *missional* life, *missional* participation... and *missional* God'.[40] Stroope's concerns echo the challenges of serving in mission in a world of complexity and multiple contexts and cultures. It may be better to describe rather than define terms. This avoids placing concepts in a box or being concrete in situations that call for flexibility. The focus is not so much on finding new words, or the right terminology, because this may leave us where we started.

As we contemplate the importance of terminology we use in and for mission, certain factors shape the words we use. This language should:

---

[37] Stroope, 14.
[38] Stroope, 14.
[39] Stroope, 19.
[40] Stroope, 20.

- reflect the 'bigness', the grandeur, the vastness of scope of God's mission;
- draw widely from Scripture in demonstrating how God's people have always been drawn into God's mission;
- demonstrate that our participation is much broader than the sending aspect of mission;
- emphasise the central role of local communities of believers in mission, however fragile they may be (e.g. young churches, small numbers of Christians, or contexts of hostility);
- enable all God's people to find their place in his mission;
- affirm that relationship is primary, and task flows out of these relationships.

Diverse Images of the People of God in Mission

The Bible employs a rich variety of imagery to describe the people of God, which in turn inspires and empowers multiple approaches to mission and faithful witness. Drawing on deeper insights into biblical imagery helps us respond to the disruptive movement of God in his people and the global church today. Our aim in this chapter is to help motivate the reader to reflect on the relevance of this imagery, applying their insights to their own missional context more thoroughly.

John Driver, in *Images of the Church in Mission*, discusses the importance of how

> images serve to communicate the church's self-understanding; they are also powerful forces for creating an authentic sense of identity and mission… However, images need to be understood in their formative settings, in their social and religious contexts of origin. Then they are a powerful resource for calling God's people back to their roots in God's saving intentions for his people and for all humanity.[41]

To set the stage for exploring biblical imagery, we use various types of concepts that include illustrative language. Let us explore some of the main types.

Imagery is 'the use of words or pictures in books, films, paintings, etc. to describe ideas or situations'.[42] Biblical examples are in Revelation 9:11, where 'John borrows Joel's imagery here (e.g. Joel 1:6; 2:4-5) to amplify the imagery of a locust plague into a terrible invasion'.[43]

Figurative language is a creative form of expression that doesn't use a word's literal meaning. It is commonly used in comparisons and exaggerations, and to convey complex ideas. For instance, when someone mentions having 'butterflies in their stomach' because they are nervous, they are not implying the presence of actual butterflies inside them; rather, they are using figurative language to

---

[41] John Driver, *Images of the Church in Mission* (Scottdale: Herald Press, 1997), 17.
[42] "Imagery," accessed 30 January 2022,
https://dictionary.cambridge.org/dictionary/english/imagery.
[43] Craig Keener, *The IVP Bible Background Commentary New Testament*, 2nd ed. (Downers Grove: IVP Academic, 2014), 747.

describe the sensation of unease. In John 4:15, Jesus encounters the Samaritan woman at the well:

> The images of water and wells were often used symbolically in antiquity; like many other characters in John, however, she takes Jesus literally when he is speaking figuratively. Nonwealthy rural women usually went to nearby water sources to draw water; they could let down their pitcher or other vessel into a spring, and sometimes would carry it back on their head.[44]

There are common types of figurative language:

Simile makes direct comparisons, using the words 'like' or 'as'. When Jesus said that the kingdom of God is like a mustard tree (Mark 4:30), he uses the literary device of a simile to help us understand something vague (the kingdom of God) with something more tangible (mustard seed).

Metaphor: George Lakoff and Mark Johnson in their book *Metaphors We Live By* state that 'The essence of metaphor is understanding and experiencing one kind of thing in terms of another.'[45] Metaphors make indirect comparisons that form a connection in the reader's mind, even if the objects being compared are not necessarily similar. John Driver notes how 'Metaphorical language can communicate more powerfully and imaginatively than abstract language... Images serve to communicate the church's self-understanding; they are also powerful forces for creating an authentic sense of identity and mission.'[46] Consider this example in Luke 17:1-2 (NLT): 'Jesus said to his disciples, "There will always be temptations to sin, but what sorrow awaits the person who does the tempting!"' Craig Keener notes 'those who caused others to stumble ("to sin" – ESV, NLT) are as doomed as the rich man of the preceding parable'.[47] Keener states that '"Stumble" was often used metaphorically to refer to sinning or falling away from the true faith.'[48] Two other examples are how 'Jewish teachers often used "stumbling" as a metaphor for sin'[49] and in 1 Thessalonians 4:4, '"Vessel" (KJV, NASB) was commonly used as a metaphor for one's "body"'.[50]

Personification attributes human characteristics to nonhuman or abstract entities, encompassing physical attributes ('the eye of the needle'), emotional attributes ('a single lonely shoe'), or human actions ('a leaf dancing in the wind'). In Romans 8:39, '"height" and "depth" may well simply personify the heavens above and Hades (the realm of death) below (cf. Ps. 139:8); taken together, this was a good Jewish way to encompass all creation (cf. Isa. 7:11)'.[51]

Hyperbole is a powerful tool of exaggeration that amplifies a sentiment for emphasis, often stretching beyond the bounds of realism. For example, in the gospels, Craig Keener states 'The point of Jesus' hyperbolic illustrations is

---

44 Keener, 259.
45 George Lakoff, and Mark Johson, *Metaphors We Live By* (Chicago, IL: University of Chicago Press, 2003), 5.
46 Driver, 17.
47 Keener, 225.
48 Keener, 225.
49 Keener, 676.
50 Keener, 587.
51 Keener, 442.

generally to grab the hearer's attention and force that hearer to take his point seriously.'[52] In Luke 18:25-27, Jesus' saying 'reflects a Jewish figure of speech for doing something impossible (a large animal going through a needle's eye). The saying, a hyperbole, uses the image of a literal needle (not a gate, as some have incorrectly thought).'[53]

Allusion suggests a familiar person, work, event, or popular culture reference. It relies on common knowledge, requiring no further explanation. For example, Matthew 17:1-13 has 'many allusions to God revealing his glory to Moses on Mount Sinai that most ancient Jewish readers would certainly have caught'.[54]

Analogy is 'a comparison between things that have similar features, often used to help explain a principle or idea'.[55] In Luke 4:25-27, Elijah and Elisha are appropriate 'analogies for Jesus' ministry, which included raising the dead and multiplying food (similar to what Elijah did for the widow of Zarephath) and healing lepers'.[56]

Symbolism uses symbols, which are objects, actions, or concepts that represent or embody deeper meanings, often beyond their literal interpretation. Symbols convey abstract ideas or emotions evocatively, allowing for layers of interpretation and enriching an overall message. In Luke 22:19-20, Jesus uses bread to represent his body and wine as his shed blood. Christians continue this practice of symbolism in celebrating communion. Craig Keener presents some symbolism that John uses in Revelation:

> As in the Old Testament prophets, much of John's symbolic language is meant as evocative imagery, to elicit particular responses, rather than as a detailed literal picture of events. Readers steeped in the Old Testament and Jewish apocalyptic literature would have understood this method of interpretation; sometimes older symbols could be reapplied to new situations but were meant to evoke the same sort of response. Sometimes John simply explains what the symbols mean (e.g. 1:20); in other cases, the first readers would have understood from other clues in his book or because of cultural information or knowledge of how these symbols were used in antiquity, which he and his readers both understood. John plainly expected his readers to understand his points (1:3; 22:10).[57]

Word picture is 'a description in words, especially one that is unusually vivid'.[58] For example, in Matthew 3:11-12, John the Baptist used word pictures of fire that he connects with the activity of the Holy Spirit (v.11) and as burning up chaff from the wheat (v.12).

---

[52] Keener, 782.

[53] Keener, 228.

[54] Keener, 88.

[55] "Analogy," accessed 30 January 2022, https://dictionary.cambridge.org/dictionary/english/analogy.

[56] Keener, 191.

[57] Keener, 726.

[58] "Word picture," accessed 30 January 2022, https://www.dictionary.com/browse/word-picture.

Parable: To provoke and gain the attention of his audience, Jesus used many stories, similes (as comparisons), and riddles in the form of his parables. Most theologians agree that there are 38 parables from Jesus in the gospels. Some repeat the same message, some have many interpretations, and several point to the future. Jesus' parables are unique because they're his words straight from his mouth. In other words, Jesus' parables were attention-grabbing stories that piqued the interest of the listeners and were relatable so people could understand the objects and situations in the parables. This helped them connect with Jesus' message and grasp spiritual lessons which conceal deeper wisdom for those genuinely seeking the truth. They would study and ponder the parables to find wisdom in them.

For example, in one grouping of parables, Jesus emphasises alertness, readiness, and accountability. Faithful followers are called to be watchful for Jesus' return (Mark 13:32-37 and Luke 12:35-40). In the parable of the net (Matt. 13:47-50) and the parable of the sheep and goats (Matt. 25:31-46), Jesus teaches about a coming judgement and a separation of the faithful righteous and the unfaithful unrighteous at the end. In the parable of the fig tree (Matt. 24:32-35, Mark 13:28-29, and Luke 21:29-31), the point is to be aware of the times one lives in and prepare for Jesus' return.

Imagery of the Church *in* Mission

So far, we have focused on the rich diversity of types of language of communication used within Scripture. We build upon this as we consider imagery from the Bible that gives us fresh insights about the people of God in mission in the context of the global church. A fruitful way to explore this is to consider the many metaphors and images used to describe the people of God and ask in what ways these may help us understand the nature of the church in mission today.

John Driver notes how the Bible uses nearly 100 different images for the church.[59] He also observes how the church tends to form its self-perception from images in secular society rather than relying on the New Testament. While the church has largely retained its traditional images to describe its identity and purpose, these images have been detached from their original context and distorted from their intended meaning.[60] Driver states that 'the biblical images of the church can only be radically understood in a church committed to be God's contrast society in the world'.[61] This necessitates approaching biblical images with 'authentic and intentional naivete' as we align with the values of God's kingdom, which is 'essential if we are going to break out of the stranglehold of the world's inverted system of values'.[62]

---

[59] Driver, 9.
[60] Driver, 18.
[61] Driver, 22.
[62] Driver, 22.

An example of imagery of the church in mission, as used in the New Testament, is 'the way'. Driver remarks that this 'must have been one of the Christian community's earliest self-designations'.[63] Some examples: 'prepare the way of the Lord' (Luke 3:4 referring to Isa. 40:3); Jesus' teaching about two ways (Matt. 7:13-14); Jesus as the 'new and living way' (Heb. 9:8-14; 10:19-25); those who 'belonged to the way' (Acts 9:1-2); and the example of Felix, who was 'rather well informed about the Way' (Acts 24:22).[64]

In the Old Testament, 'way' is also used in a variety of places: Jethro's advice to Moses to teach the Israelites 'decrees and instructions' is so that they will see 'the way they are to live and how they are to behave' (Exod. 18:20). God's people are commanded to 'ask where the good way is, and walk in it' (Jer. 6:16). The wise person walks 'in the way of righteousness' (Prov. 8:20). David the psalmist takes notice of the 'way of integrity' (Ps. 101:2, 6). Further, David desired to be led by God 'in the everlasting way' (Ps. 139:24).[65]

Driver also mentions this background to the way imagery: in Mark 1:3, 'the way of the Lord' is 'a new exodus' (Exod. 3:20) with John's announcement 'of a new messianic era'.[66] In Isaiah 40:3, the prophet calls for the preparation for God's salvation: 'A voice of one calling, "in the desert prepare the way for the Lord, make straight in the wilderness a highway for our God".' This is Mark's introduction to John's ministry as the one preparing the way for the Messiah. Driver sees the roots of this in the Exodus language. In various references to walking on the way to Jerusalem (e.g. Matt. 20:17), they provide a context 'for Jesus to instruct his followers in the meaning and realities of discipleship'.[67] In the parable of the two ways in Matthew 7:13-14 and Luke 13:23-24, 'Jesus concludes summaries of the substance of discipleship with an invitation to enter the "narrow gate" and to take the "hard road".'[68] When Jesus said, 'I am the Way' (John 14:6), his disciples knew what he was talking about – 'he was the authentic way to access God'.[69] Through Jesus' obedient death, he became 'the new and living way' as the old covenant was replaced with the new (Heb. 9:8-14; 10:19-25).[70] Finally, Christ-followers are encouraged to 'walk in the way of love' (Eph. 5:2), to live as Christ did (1 John 2:6), and to 'live a life worthy of the Lord and please him in every way' (Col. 1:10).[71]

The imagery of 'the way' holds significance to the church that lives under the shadow of the cross and a church that bears witness through suffering. When these aspects are missing, the imagery itself loses its captivating power.[72]

---

[63] Driver, 46.
[64] Driver, 46–47.
[65] Driver, 48–49.
[66] Driver, 50.
[67] Driver, 51.
[68] Driver, 52.
[69] Driver, 52.
[70] Driver, 54.
[71] Driver, 54.
[72] Driver, 55.

Driver's description of imagery of the way is just one part of his category of 'Pilgrimage Images' that also includes sojourners and the poor. His other categories are: 'New-Order Images' of the kingdom of God, new creation, and new humanity; 'Peoplehood Images' of the people of God, the family of God, the shepherd and the flock; and 'Images of Transformation' that are salt, light, a city, a spiritual house, and a witnessing community.[73]

Imagery of the People of God in Mission

Christopher Wright in *The Mission of God's People* notes the 'challenges and responsibilities' that we as the people of God experience in finding our place in the biblical story.[74] Wright points out that the whole world constitutes the goal of God's mission, and therefore the whole world is the scope of our mission and the arena in which we participate in mission.[75] Wright groups his work under macro themes that connect God's mission to biblical texts and our participation in his mission as God's people. Wright draws from the Old and New Testaments to gain insights about who Christians are and what they are here for. We've rephrased Wright's descriptions as imagery of people serving in God's mission who demonstrate the following traits:

- Actors: 'Know the story they are part of' – they recognise that they live in the space from the first creation to the new creation. They are 'God's co-workers' (1 Cor. 3:9) and this gives a sense of 'irrepressible optimism' based on 'the promise of God' who makes everything new (Rev. 21:3-5).[76]

- Stewards: 'Care for creation' – they understand that because 'creation is one of the major themes in biblical theology', and as 'redeemed humanity', they have a responsibility to be steward-servants of what God has put them in charge of (Gen. 1:26-28). This is part of what it means to be human and participate in God's 'ecological mission'.[77]

- A Blessing: 'Are a blessing to the nations' – they appreciate how, from Abraham onward, 'God intends to bless all nations' (Gen. 12:1-3). This means that they 'inherit Abraham's blessing' and therefore his God-given mission 'to go and be a blessing... to others'.[78]

- 'Walk in God's way' – they commit to 'be the community who live by the ethical standards of the ways of God' because they understand how, from Abraham onward (Gen. 18:19), God calls his people to live with integrity, righteousness, and justice. This is part of living with the realisation that 'ethics and God's mission are integrally bound together'.[79]

---

[73] Driver, 6–7.
[74] Wright, 47.
[75] Wright, 26–27.
[76] Wright, 35–44.
[77] Wright, 62.
[78] Wright, 61–84.
[79] Wright, 82–95.

- Redeemed: 'Are redeemed for redemptive living' – they appreciate how the Book of Exodus gives a 'model for behaviour [for] redeemed people' in a 'holistic or integral understanding of mission' that covers 'social, political, economic concern[s] and action alongside the spiritual dimension of personal forgiveness'.[80]
- Representatives: 'Represent God to the world' – they live within God's story, starting in the Old Testament and the people of Israel through to the completion of the story. They understand how the mission of the people of God (1 Pet. 2:9-12) 'lies between the past and the future, between grace and glory, between historical salvation and ongoing mission, between what God has done and will do'.[81]
- Magnets: 'Attract others to God' – they comprehend that being God's people in mission means 'to have God so much at the centre of what they are, and they do' (Titus 2:9-10). This becomes the space of 'missional magnetism' where 'God's own gravitational pull… draws people into the sphere of his blessing'.[82]
- Confidants: 'Know the one living God and saviour' – they understand that God wants to be known and 'this is what makes our mission not only imperative but possible'. This is also difficult because mission takes place among competing loyalties. However, they are confident that the Bible and the gospel of Christ that they share 'is good news about real events' (Acts 3:15, 4:2, 9-10, 16).[83]
- Witnesses: 'Bear witness to the living God' – they know that gospel witness comes from the 'gospel transformation' of their own lives (Matt. 28:19-20). They 'speak up for him when opportunities arise'. They experience how the 'act of bearing witness… generates… conviction' to continue to witness (Isa. 43:10).[84]
- Town-criers: 'Proclaim the gospel of Christ' – they understand that 'the mission of God's people is to bring *good* news to a world where *bad* news is depressingly endemic'. They announce the gospel because they know it 'must be heard' (Eph. 1:13) and 'preached to all nations'.[85]
- On the move: 'Send and are sent' – they participate in the 'authorizing, commissioning, sending action of the saving God'. This means they are 'caught up within the dynamic sending and being sent' that the triune God 'has done and continues to do for the salvation of the world and the revelation of his truth' (3 John 8).[86]
- Participants: 'Live and work in the public square' – they understand how 'work is God's idea', 'the task of ruling the earth (Gen. 1), and of serving and

---

[80] Wright, 96–113.

[81] Wright, 114–27.

[82] Wright, 128–47.

[83] Wright, 151–62.

[84] Wright, 163–78.

[85] Wright, 179–200.

[86] Wright, 201–21.

keeping it (Gen. 2)'. This requires '*constructive engagement* in the world' and '*courageous confrontation* with the world'. One's 'daily work matters because it matters to God' and therefore living and working as Christ's disciples has missional impact.[87]

• Worshippers: 'Praise and prayer' – they know they 'were created to bring praise and glory to God and to bring the nations of the world into the same orchestra of doxology' (Rev. 5:13). The missional aspect is that the people of God 'bring glory to God our creator... in the midst of the nations who do not yet know God as creator and redeemer' because 'worship and witness are closely intertwined' (Ps. 96).[88]

Imagery of the Body of Christ

Paul Minear in *Images of the Church in the New Testament* categorises 'minor images' and 'major images' of the church. He identifies 32 minor images including: salt of the earth (Matt. 5:13), a letter from Christ (2 Cor. 3:2-3), fish and fish net (Mark 1:17, Matt. 4:19, Luke 5:1-11), the boat (Matt. 8:23-27), the ark (a comparison to the days of Noah) (Matt. 24:36-42), unleavened bread (Matt. 16:6), one loaf (1 Cor. 10:16-17), the table of the Lord (1 Cor. 10:21), the altar (Heb. 13:10), the cup of the Lord (1 Cor. 10:16), wine (Mark 2:22), branches of the vine (John 15), vineyard (1 Cor. 9:7), the fig tree (Luke 13:6-9), the olive tree (Rom. 11:13-24), God's planting (1 Cor. 3:9), God's building (1 Cor. 3:9), building on the rock (Matt. 16:18-19), pillar and buttress (1 Tim. 3:5, 15), virgins (Rev. 14:1-4, Matt. 25:1-13), the Messiah's mother (Rev. 12:1-2), the elect lady (2 John 1:1), the bride of Christ (2 Cor. 11:1f), the wedding feast (Rev. 19:9 and Mark 2:19), the wearers of white robes (Rev. 19:7, Matt. 22:1-14), the choice of clothing (Rom. 13:14), citizens (Eph. 2:19, Gal. 6:10), exiles (1 Pet. 1:1, 2:11), the dispersion (Jas. 1:1, 1 Pet. 1:1), ambassadors (2 Cor. 5:18-21), the poor (Luke 6:20), and hosts and guests (Matt. 25:31-46).[89]

Minear gives this example of the image of the dispersion:

> ... by the first century the Diaspora seems to have become a technical term among the Jews to refer to those Jews who were living outside the homeland. Christians made little use of it as such. But the less technical idea that the faithful people would be scattered until the Messiah should come and that his salvation would take the form of a final gathering of the scattered sheep was much more congenial, although at the same time more fluid.[90]

Minear identifies a further 50 major images that he gathers into three groups:

(1) 'Images that gravitate around the conception of the church as the people of God.'[91] These connect the contemporary Christian generation to the historic

---

[87] Wright, 222–43.
[88] Wright, 244–62.
[89] Paul S. Minear, *Images of the Church in the New Testament* (Philadelphia: Westminister, 1960), 29–65.
[90] Minear, 62.
[91] Minear, 67.

biblical community 'whose origin stemmed from God's covenant promises and whose pilgrimage has been sustained by God's call'.[92]

(2) 'Images that gravitate around the activity of God in creating a new humanity' (i.e. the new creation).[93] The function of these images 'is to see the life of the Christian society within the context of God's eternal glory and life, and therefore within the context of the redemption of the world'.[94]

(3) 'Images that gravitate around the conception of the church as a fellowship in faith.'[95] This describes a community of God's people who share an interdependence of giving and calling in this fellowship.

Minear also identifies a set of terms relating to 'the body of Christ', through the interrelated pictures of body, members, and head. While terms like people, family, flock, and citizenship all have their origins in the Old Testament, the body of Christ imagery is only found in the New Testament in the writings of Paul. Minear states 'the phrase "the body of Christ" is not a single expression with an unchanging meaning. Paul's thought remains extremely flexible and elastic.'[96] Therefore, this diversity of usage, Minear says, 'should warn us against seeking to produce a single inclusive definition of the image, and against importing into each occurrence of the analogy the range of meanings which it bears in other passages'.[97] The range of usage cited by Minear includes: 'the bodies of the saints as members of Christ', 'partnership in the Body and the blood', 'the diversities of ministries in one body' (e.g. 'the spiritual body' and 'the head of the body'), the 'head… of the elemental cosmic spirits', 'the head of the church', 'the body of this head', 'the unity of Jews and Gentiles', 'the growth of the body', and the 'fullness of God'.[98]

Minear intends for the reader to appreciate the interconnectedness of all these images while appreciating the original intent of the authors. The images relate to one another and form a unified whole. They overlap and interchange with each other. Minear notes, 'only the power of the Spirit in Christ to knit a community together in love can enable men to know the knowledge-surpassing dimensions of the fullness of God'.[99]

Imagery of the Church *and* Mission

Donald Senior notes how biblical images of church and images of mission are closely interconnected: 'One's understanding of mission shapes one's operative understanding of what the church is meant to be.'[100] Senior wants us to reflect and 'probe to the underlying values and assumptions that underwrite a particular

---

[92] Minear, 67.

[93] Minear, 67.

[94] Minear, 67.

[95] Minear, 67.

[96] Minear, 173.

[97] Minear, 174.

[98] Minear, 178–213.

[99] Minear, 220.

[100] Senior, 3.

image'.[101] These images provide the church with 'biblically sanctioned modes of mission'.[102] But, they also show 'the dynamic tension between identity and outreach, between community and mission, between particularism and universality' that are seen in the Bible and therefore 'cannot be reduced to a simple formula' but they do help 'bring coherence' to our understanding of the church and mission.[103]

Senior provides 'three dominant images of church and mission which are linked in the New Testament materials':[104]

(1) 'A "sending" church conceived of as a community of disciples or as a pilgrim, itinerant church whose mission is to cross boundaries and to proclaim the gospel to the entire world';

(2) 'A "witnessing" church whose mission is to give credible witness to the world through its manifest faith and its virtue';

(3) 'A "receptive" church whose mission is expressed in its very being as a hospitable and inclusive community of healing, reconciliation, and unity.'[105]

Senior provides a grid to assist us in appreciating the biblical imagery of the church in mission in the New Testament. We have adapted it in Table 9.

Image of Church	Image of Mission	Dominant Theology Christology	Goal	Texts
I. Community of sent disciples	Urgent itinerant proclamation of the gospel to the world	God as sovereign; Christ triumphant; Saviour of the world; apocalyptic	To convert and save	Rom. 15:14-21; Mark 13; Matt. 28:16-20
II. Community of visible witness	Personal and communal witness leading to persuasion, challenge, conversion	God as holy and sanctifying; Christ as prophet and teacher	To inspire, challenge, transform	1 Pet.; Rev.; Acts 2, 4; John 13-15

---

[101] Senior, 4.
[102] Senior, 4.
[103] Senior, 5.
[104] Senior, 7.
[105] Senior, 7.

| III. Community of healing and reconciliation | Proclamation of the gospel of healing and forgiveness | God as unifying and healing/saving (eschato-logical) | To build community, reconcile, unite | Matt. 18; Luke 15; John 17; Eph. 2; Luke 4; Mark 3, 6 |

Table 9: Dominant Images of Church and Mission in the New Testament

Senior provides an explanation of the above through these categories:[106]

(1) *Urgent itinerant proclamation of the gospel to the world.* Paul's church imagery aligns with his mission as a band of travelling and empowered followers sent beyond their community's boundaries for the urgent proclamation of the gospel to the world. Early Christians imitated Jesus' itinerant lifestyle, devoting themselves to announcing God's radical message. Now, the church serves as a community of disciples, trained by Jesus, and sent to cross-cultural boundaries, proclaiming the gospel.

(2) *Personal and communal witness leading to persuasion, challenge, and conversion.* Early Christians were called to be holy (1 Pet. 1:15) and distinct from the immoral behaviour of the surrounding unbelievers (1 Pet. 4:3-4). Christians are born anew and valued by God, even if rejected by their peers. The community is likened to a temple built with living stones, and they are chosen to proclaim God's praises and bring others out of darkness (1 Pet. 2:4-5). The church is also tasked with the mission of witnessing to their faith, seeking to win over non-believers. This underlying theology emphasises a Christian's and the church community's call to holiness, setting them apart from the world while demonstrating love, integrity, and service as a testimony to God's holiness and the truth of the gospel to a potentially hostile world (1 Pet. 2:9).

(3) *Proclamation of the gospel of healing and forgiveness.* The healing ministry of Jesus, portrayed in the synoptic gospels, is an important backdrop for mission. Jesus' encounters with people are often associated with healing, breaking boundaries, and addressing various dimensions of human experience. In Ephesians (2:14), Jesus' mission is described as a historic reconciliation, breaking down the enmity between Jew and Gentile. In the New Testament, the church is a sacred temple, a dwelling place of God in the Spirit. The church is a healing and reconciling community that welcomes outsiders who seek life within the faith community. The church is seen as a sacrament of ultimate unity, reflecting the unity prayed for by Jesus. The goal of the church's mission is unity in God's love, demonstrated through humble service and self-sacrificing love.

One of Senior's significant contributions is to propose that while there are three major ways in which the church understood its mission portrayed in the New Testament, each understanding of mission was shaped by the specific

---

[106] Senior, 7–15.

context in which the church found itself. Today, the global church exists in hugely diverse contexts, including diverse worldviews and religions, secularism and pluralism, wealth and poverty, relative stability and war, the ravages of climate change and migration. As we have seen, the Bible offers us an extraordinary range of images of the people of God in mission. As the church in different contexts develops its Mission Theology, we would expect different images to be most relevant to each context. The days of the Christendom paradigm of mission, with its Mission Theology resting on the singular image of the apostolic band, are giving way to a range of mission theologies that draw on the richness of the biblical narrative. There is work to be done to fully harness the wealth of the biblical images of the people of God in mission. The more different parts of the global church can engage in the development of their own Mission Theology, the more we will all grow in the understanding of our place in God's mission.

Summary

The importance of the language of mission requires consideration because how we talk about God's mission influences our missional identity and practice. The words of mission that we use 'shape and express belief and ideals, choices and purpose'.[107] We've discovered how the term 'mission' is everywhere in our vocabulary. When we look closer at it and include its specialised and technical uses, it can appear 'complex and often bewildering'.[108] This applies to any of the terms we use associated with mission (e.g. missional, missionary, *missio Dei*). They are used in such a wide way that we can pass nearly every missiological and theological concern and issue through them. In doing so, their meaning becomes murkier. Therefore, Stroope encourages us to explore this more deeply because 'our pioneering task is to transcend mission and to discover fresh impulse and renewed vision for witness to the gospel of Jesus Christ'.[109]

We also explored a range of biblical imagery and examples of the people of God and the church of God in mission. We noted how John Driver, Christopher Wright, Paul Minear, and Donald Senior provide us with insights that inform, inspire, and empower mission. The different images help us understand what kind of witness is most appropriate for the wide range of contexts in which the global church finds itself today. The dominant mission paradigm has tended to reduce mission to one or two approaches. However, through the range of biblical imagery about the people of God and church in mission, we can see how the Scriptures open the possibility of a much richer and more diverse way of understanding our call.

---

[107] Stroope, xiii.

[108] Stroope, 1.

[109] Stroope, 30.

Reflective Questions:

- The terms mission, missions, missionary, and missional have many meanings and implications. What stands out from our overview of their theological development and modern use? Do you need to modify how you use any of these terms? If so, how?
- What insights and implications from the biblical imagery bring fresh perspectives when applied to contexts of mission?

Conclusion

We set out to write an introductory book about Mission Theology, focusing on the connection between theology and practice, because we saw the need for a book that could serve mission and church leaders and practitioners. Through the pages of this book, we've explored the foundation for Mission Theology. The terminology of mission has implications, and we mentioned some of these. We explored mission through a series of historical, biblical, and current contexts – all through the perspective of the Protestant mission. Mission Theology is a multidisciplinary study and is integral rather than peripheral to all theology because it assists us in questioning and clarifying assumptions of historical, sociological, and contextual factors, theological issues, and expectations of mission practice, such as theology, biblical studies, and social sciences.

One of the disciplines we examined is the newer field of missional hermeneutics. Using examples from the Book of Job, the Gospel of John and the epistles of Colossians and Ephesians, we explored how theologians who've worked with these books have helped us read them with a missional perspective. This is necessary to keep us from proof-texting the Scriptures by finding a Bible passage supporting our missional perspective. Instead, we are encouraged to read the Bible through a missional hermeneutic matrix because Mission Theology is derived from the narrative of the whole Scripture.

The triune missionary God is the source for Mission Theology. All three members of the Trinity are purposely involved in and lead in God's mission. The triune God's mission and his plan is for everyone and everything to be brought together under the Lordship of Christ. Reflecting the nature of the relationship of the triune God, God's people are called from and into their contexts to bring the whole gospel to the whole world.

The Integrated Missiological Matrix brings together four important dimensions of mission: the Bible, Church, Personal Pilgrimage, and Context. This tool can be useful in any context of mission because, every time we use it, it reminds us that mission is multidimensional.

The theological development of the concept of the *missio Dei* and how it has been interpreted through recent church history has been explored in this book. This journey raised concerns about the language of mission, which shapes identity, belief, and ideals about participating in God's mission. The potential vagueness of the language we use in mission means *missio Dei* can become a conduit by which nearly any issue associated with mission can be included. The language of mission has power and influences our understanding of the triune God's intentions and actions in redeeming all his creation.

We looked at six church and mission history paradigms over the past 2,000 years. Each paradigm took time, even centuries, to emerge and become the new norm. These six paradigms help us better understand Christendom's effect on modern mission. However, of greater interest is the unforeseen Christian century of global mission. The impact of a thousand years of Christendom has seen the Western form of Christianity lose its predominant place in global Christianity and its leadership of the modern missionary movement of the past 200 years. As history has progressed, we noted at times how the church and mission agencies could sound triumphant because of Christendom's influence on the progress of mission. However, we noted how Christianity is not subject to predictable progress, and its power is not human-made but belongs to God.

The use of biblical imagery about the people of God in mission, developed through the work of several theologians, provides insights that inform how we engage with the biblical text, theological traditions, and contexts of mission. In particular, it inspires us to envision the reality of the global church.

As the twenty-first century progresses, the global church paradigm is well underway and not built by powerful institutions. Even so, we see ongoing disparities and imbalances between the two paradigms of Christendom and the global church. The former has had a thousand years of confidence and strength. The latter is still forming and, in comparison, can be perceived as in its adolescent stage. The Western world has led the modern missionary movement of the past 200 years. Therefore, intentional efforts are necessary to overcome the gaps between these two paradigms. This is critical, since mission originates from God, not churches and institutions of either paradigm. God's focus is on his kingdom where *shalom*, the redemption and renewal of the whole creation, is fulfilled. Mission involves the whole church of both paradigms, since the entire church is called to bear witness to God's purposes and activities, fulfilled in Jesus Christ.

This book is our appeal for all of us who are involved in and lead in God's mission to think more deeply and theologically about it to be better equipped to respond biblically to very diverse, dynamic, and changing contexts. The changing local, regional, and global contexts require us to adjust and change our mission methodologies, emphasising friendship, partnership, and generosity. Some methods may have a short lifespan, while others may be more durable. When change is necessary, missional practitioners must have the courage to adjust without compromising biblical insights or integrity. Engaging with Mission Theology in all its richness will enable us to be better positioned to improve and strengthen mission theory and praxis in whatever area or sphere God calls for our contribution. We hope you will continue to grow as a reflective practitioner who embraces integrity, creativity, openness, and curiosity in participating in God's mission.

Bibliography

Adeney, Miram. "Algeria." In *Evangelical Dictionary of World Missions*. Edited by A. Scott Moreau. Grand Rapids: Baker, 2000.

Aldridge, Boone. *For the Gospel's Sake: The Rise of Wycliffe Bible Translators and the Summer Institute of Linguistics*. Grand Rapids: Wm B. Eerdmans, 2018.

Balia, Daryl, and Kirsteen Kim. *Witnessing to Christ Today*. Oxford: Regnum, 2010.

Bandura, Albert. "Toward an Agentic Theory of the Self." *Advances in Self Research* 3 (2008).

Barrett, David. *God's Word Alone: The Authority of Scripture*. Grand Rapids: Zondervan, 2016.

Bauckman, Richard. "Bible and Mission: The Modern/Postmodern Western Context." In *Bible in Mission*. Edited by Pauline Hoggarth, Fergus Macdonald, Bill Mitchell, and Knud Jørgensen. Oxford: Regnum, 2013.

Bediako, Kwame. "The African Renaissance and Theological Reconstruction: The Challenge of the Twenty-First Century." *Journal of African Christian Thought* 4, no. 2 (2001): 29–33.

Bendor-Samuel, Paul. "Challenge and Realignment in the Protestant Cross-Cultural Mission Movement." *Transformation* 34, no. 4 (2017).

Bevans, Stephen, and Roger Schroeder. *Constants in Context: A Theology for Mission Today*. Maryknoll: Orbis Books, 2004.

Bliese, Richard. "The Mission Matrix: Mapping Out the Complexities of a Missional Ecclesiology." *Word & World* 26, no. 3 (2006).

Bosch, David. *Transforming Mission: Paradigm Shifts in Theology of Mission*. Maryknoll: Orbis Books, 1991.

Bosch, David. *Transforming Mission: Paradigm Shifts in Theology of Mission*. Maryknoll: Orbis Books, 2011.

Burden, Matthew. *Missionary Motivations: Challenges from the Early Church*. Littleton: William Carey Publishing, 2023.

Bush, Luis. "AD2000 and Beyond: Toward a Conceptual Model." In *Working Together With God to Shape the New Milliennium: Opportunities and Limitations*. Edited by Gary Corwin and Kenneth Mulholland. Pasadena: William Carey Library, 2000.

Cardoza-Orlandi, Carlos F., and Justo L. Gonzáles. *To All Nations, From All Nations: A History of the Christian Missionary Movement*. Nashville: Abingdon Press, 2013.

Carr, Burgess. "The Engagement of Lusaka." *Pro Veritate* (June 1974).

Carson, D.A. "Domesticating the Gospel: A Review of Grenz's Renewing the Center." In *Reclaiming the Center: Confronting Evangelical*

Accommodation in Postmodern Times. Edited by Millard J. Erickson, Paul Kjoss Helseth, and Justin Taylor. Wheaton: Crossway, 2004.

Cassidy, Michael. "The Call to Moratorium: Perspective on an Identity Crisis." *Churchman* 90, no. 4 (1976): 265–80. Accessed 29 August 2020. https://churchsociety.org/docs/churchman/090/Cman_090_4_Cassidy.pdf.

Chong, Calvin. "Globalization, Hybrid Worlds, and Emerging Missional Frontiers." In *A Hybrid World: Diaspora, Hybridity, and Missio Dei*. Edited by Sadiri Joy Tira and Juliet Lee Uytanlet. Littleton: William Carey Publishing, 2020.

Corrie, John. *Dictionary of Mission Theology: Evangelical Foundations*. Edited by John Corrie. Downers Grove: IVP Academic, 2007.

Das, Rupen. "What the Majority World Is Saying about Mission Today." *Evangelical Review of Theology* 46, no. 3 (2022).

Davy, Tim J. *The Book of Job and the Mission of God: A Missional Reading*. Eugene: Pickwick Publications, 2020.

Dilley, Andrea Palpant. "The World the Missionaries Made." *Christianity Today*, 2014.

Dowsett, Rose. *The Cape Town Commitment Study Edition*. Peabody: Hendrickson Publishers, 2012.

Driver, John. *Images of the Church in Mission*. Scottdale: Herald Press, 1997.

Escobar, Samuel. "Managerial Missiology." In *Dictionary of World Mission*. Edited by John Corrie. Downers Grove: IVP Academic, 2007.

Escobar, Samuel. *The New Global Mission: The Gospel From Everywhere to Everyone*. Downers Grove: InterVarsity Press, 2003.

Flemming, Dean. "A Missional Reading of Colossians." In *Reading the Bible Missionally*. Edited by Michael Goheen. Grand Rapids: Wm B. Eerdmans, 2016.

Flett, John. *The Witness of God: The Trinity, Missio Dei, Karl Barth, and the Nature of Christian Community*. Grand Rapids: Wm B. Eerdmans, 2010.

Francis, Pope. *Apostolic Exhortation Evangelii Gaudium*. The Vatican: Vatican Press, 2013.

Franke, John R. "Intercultural Hermeneutics and the Shape of Missional Theology." In *Reading the Bible Missionally*. Edited by Michael Goheen. Grand Rapids: Wm B. Eerdmans, 2016, Kindle edition.

Franke, John R. *Missional Theology: An Introduction*. Grand Rapids: Baker Academic, 2020.

Franklin, Kirk. "Implications of Identity in Global Mission." *Missiology: An International Review* 51, no. 1 (2023): 74–84. https://dx.doi.org/10.1177/00918296221117709.

Franklin, Kirk. *Towards Global Missional Leadership*. Oxford: Regnum Books International, 2017.

Franklin, Kirk, and Nelus Niemandt. "Funding God's Mission: Towards a Missiology of Generosity." *Missionalia* 43, no. 3 (2015).

Fung, Patrick. "Mission Partnership in a Polycentric World." In *Majority World Perspectives on Christian Mission*. Edited by Eugene Baron and Nico Botha. Auckland Park: University of Johannesburg Press, 2022.

Gailey, Charles, and Howard Culbertson. *Discovering Missions*. Kansas City: Beacon Hill Press, 2007.

Gallagher, Robert. "Missionary Methods: St Paul's, St Rolland's, or Ours?" In *Missionary Methods: Research, Reflections, and Realities*. Edited by Craig Ott and J.D. Payne. Pasadena: William Carey Library, 2013.

Gatũ, John. *Fan into Flame: An Autobiography*. Nairobi: Moran Publishers, 2016.

George, Sam. "Motus Dei (The Move of God)." In *Global Migration & Christian Faith: Implications for Identity and Mission*. Edited by M. Daniel Carroll R. and Vincent E. Bacote. Eugene: Cascade Books, 2021.

George, Sam. "Reimagining GO and SEND Mission Paradigms for an Age of Global Migration and World Christianity." *International Bulletin of Mission Research* 47, no. 2 (2023): 251–61. https://dx.doi.org/10.1177/2396939393221120499.

Giddens, Anthony. *The Third Way*. Cambridge: Polity Press, 1998.

Glasser, Arthur. *Announcing the Kingdom*. Grand Rapids: Baker Academic, 2003.

Goheen, Michael. *The Church and its Vocation: Lesslie Newbigin's Missionary Ecclessiology*. Grand Rapids: Baker Academic, 2018.

Goheen, Michael, ed. *Reading the Bible Missionally*. Edited by Michael Goheen. Grand Rapids: Wm B. Eerdmans, 2016, Kindle edition.

Goheen, Michael. *Introducing Christian Mission Today: Scripture, History and Issues*. Downers Grove: IVP Academic, 2014.

Goheen, Michael. *A Light to the Nations: The Missional Church and the Biblical Story*. Grand Rapids: Baker Academic, 2011.

Goheen, Michael, and Jim Mullins. *The Symphony of Mission*. Grand Rapids: Baker Academic, 2019.

Green, Michael. *Evangelism in the Early Church*. Grand Rapids: Wm B. Eerdmans, 2004.

Guinness, Os. *Fit Bodies, Fat Minds: Why Evangelicals Don't Think, and What to Do About It*. Grand Rapids: Baker, 1994.

Hanciles, Jehu. *Beyond Christendom: Globalization, African Migration, and the Transformation of the West*. Maryknoll: Orbis Books, 2008.

Hanciles, Jehu. *Migration and the Making of Global Christianity*. Grand Rapids: Wm B. Eerdmans, 2021.

Hartch, Todd. *The Rebirth of Latin American Christianity*. Oxford: Oxford University Press, 2014.

Hesselgrave, David. "The Great Commission." In *Evangelical Dictionary of World Missions*. Edited by Scott Moreau. Grand Rapids: Baker Books, 2000.

Hesselgrave, David. "Preface." In *Missiology and the Social Sciences: Contributions, Cautions and Conclusions*. Edited by Rommen Ed and Gary Corwin. Pasadena: William Carey Library, 1996.

Hill, Graham, and Grace Ji-Sun Kim. *Healing Our Broken Humanity*. Downers Grove: IVP, 2018.

Holland, Tom. *Dominion: The Making of the Western Mind*. London: Little, Brown, 2019.

Hunt, Robert. *The Gospel Among the Nations: A Documentary History of Inculturation*. Maryknoll: Orbis Books, 2010.

Hunter, James Davison. *To Change the World: The Irony, Tragedy, and Possibility of Christianity in the Late Modern World*. New York: Oxford University Press, 2011.

Jacobsen, Douglas. *Global Gospel: An Introduction to Christianity on Five Continents*. Grand Rapids: Baker Academic, 2015.

Jenkins, Philip. *The Next Christendom*. 3rd ed. New York: Oxford University Press, 2011.

Jennings, Willie James. *Acts – Belief: A Theological Commentary on the Bible*. Louisville: Westminister John Knox Press, 2017.

Johnson, John. *Missing Voices: Learning to Lead Beyond Our Horizons*. Carlisle: Langham Global Library, 2019.

Jørgensen, Knud. "Foreword." In *Mission and Postmodernities*. Edited by Rolv Olsen. Oxford: Regnum Books International, 2011.

Keener, Craig. *The IVP Bible Background Commentary: New Testament*. 2nd ed. Downers Grove: IVP Academic, 2014.

Kemper, Thomas. "The *Missio Dei* in Contemporary Context." *International Bulletin of Missionary Research* 38, no. 4 (2014): 188–90.

Kerr, David, and Kenneth Ross. *Edinburgh 2010: Mission Then and Now*. Oxford: Regnum, 2009.

Keum, Jooseop. *Together Towards Life: Mission and Evangelism in Changing Landscapes*. Geneva: WCC Publications, 2013.

Kim, Kirsteen. *Joining in with the Spirit: Connecting World Church and Local Mission*. London: Epworth, 2009.

Kirk, Andrew. *What is Mission?* Minneapolis: Fortress Press, 2000.

Kreider, Alan. *The Change of Conversion and the Origin of Christendom*. Eugene: Wipf & Stock, 1999.

Kreider, Alan. *The Patient Ferment of the Early Church: The Improbable Rise of Christianity in the Roman Empire*. Grand Rapids: Baker Academic, 2016.

Kreider, Alan, and Eleanor Kreider. *Worship and Mission After Christendom*. Milton Keynes: Paternoster, 2009.

Kuhn, Thomas. *The Structure of Scientific Revolutions*. 50th anniversary ed. Chicago: University of Chicago Press, 2012.

Küng, Hans. *Theology for the Third Millennium*. New York: Anchor Books, 1988.

Kwiyani, Harvey C. "Diaspora, Hybridity and Theology." In *A Hybrid World: Diaspora, Hybridity, and Missio Dei*. Edited by Sadiri Joy Tira and Juliet Lee Uytanlet. Littleton: William Carey Publishing, 2020.

Kwiyani, Harvey C. *Multicultural Kingdom: Ethnic Diversity, Mission and the Church*. London: SCM Press, 2020.

Kwon, Sung Chan. *A Missional Reading of the Fourth Gospel: A Gospel-Driven Theology of Discipleship*. Oxford: Regnum, 2022.

Lakoff, George, and Mark Johson. *Metaphors We Live By*. Chicago, IL: University of Chicago Press, 2003.

Langmead, Ross. "What is Missiology?", *Missiology: An International Review* 42, no. 1 (2013): 67–79.

Laniak, Timothy. *Shepherds After My Own Heart: Pastoral Traditions and Leadership in the Bible*. Downers Grove: InterVarsity Press, 2006.

Lausanne Movement. *Manila Manifesto*. https://lausanne.org/content/manifesto/the-manila-manifesto.

Lausanne Movement. *Cape Town Commitment*. https://lausanne.org/content/ctc/ctcommitment.

McBeth, Leon. *The Baptist Heritage*. Nashville: Broadman, 1987.

McGavran, Donald A. *Bridges of God: A Study in the Strategy of Missions*. Eugene: Wipf & Stock Publishers, 2005.

McGrath, Alister. *Historical Theology: An Introduction to the History of Christian Thought*. 2nd ed. Oxford: Wiley, 2013.

MacMullen. *Corruption and the Decline of Rome*. New York: Yale University Press, 1988.

McNeal, Reggie. *Missional Renaissance: Changing the Scorecard for the Church*. San Francisco: Jossey-Bass, 2009.

Matenga, Jay. "A New Era of Missions." Paper presented at the Mission Interlink Conference, Melbourne, Australia, 2022.

Minear, Paul S. *Images of the Church in the New Testament*. Philadelphia: Westminister, 1960.

Nehrbass, Kenneth. *Advance Missiology: How to Study Missions in Credible and Useful Ways*. Eugene: Cascade Books, 2021.

Neill, Stephen. *Creative Tension: The Duff Lectures*. London: Edinburgh House Press, 1959.

Neill, Stephen. *A History of Christian Missions*. 2nd ed. London: Penguin, 1986.

Newbigin, Lesslie. *The Gospel in a Pluralist Society*. Grand Rapids: Wm B. Eerdmans, 1989.

Newbigin, Lesslie. *The Open Secret: An Introduction to the Theology of Mission*. Revised edition. Grand Rapids: Wm B. Eerdmans, 1995.

Noll, Mark. *Turning Points: Decisive Moments in the History of Christianity*. 3rd ed. Grand Rapids: Baker Academic, 2012.

Oborji, Francis Anekwe. *Concepts of Mission: The Evolution of Contemporary Missiology*. Maryknoll: Orbis Books, 2006.

Oborji, Francis Anekwe. *Towards African Missiology: Issues of New Language for African Christianity*. Vol. 1. Bloomington: Xlibris, 2020.

Okesson, Gregg. *A Public Missiology: How Local Churches Witness to a Complex World*. Grand Rapids: Baker Academic, 2020.

Ott, Craig. *The Church on Mission: A Biblical Vision for Transformation Among All People*. Grand Rapids: Baker Academic, 2019.

Ott, Craig. "Missionary Methods: The Questions that Still Dog Us." In *Missionary Methods: Research, Reflections and Realities*. Edited by Craig Ott and J.D. Payne. Pasadena: William Carey Library, 2013.

Pachuau, Lalsangkima. *God at Work in the World: Theology and Mission in the Global Church*. Grand Rapids: Baker Academic, 2022.

Pachuau, Lalsangkima. *World Christianity: A Historical and Theological Introduction*. Nashville: Abingdon Press, 2018.

Padilla, René. "The Mission of the Church in Light of the Kingdom of God." *Transformation* 1, no. 2 (1984): 16–20.

Payne, J.D. "Introduction." In *Missionary Methods: Research, Reflections and Realities*. Edited by Craig Ott and J.D. Payne. Pasadena: William Carey Library, 2013.

Pocock, Michael. "Introduction: An Appeal for Balance." In *Missiology and the Social Sciences: Contributions, Cautions and Conclusions*. Edited by Ed Rommen and Gary Corwin. Pasadena: William Carey Library, 1996.

Robert, Dana. *Christian Mission: How Christianity Became a World Religion*. Chichester: Wiley-Blackwell, 2009.

Robert, Dana. "Cross-Cultural Friendship in the Creation of Twentieth-Century World Christianity." *International Bulletin of Missionary Research* 35, no. 2 (2011): 100–107.

Rodin, R. Scott. "A Vision for the Generous Life." In *Christ-Centered Generosity: Global Perspectives on the Biblical Call to a Generous Life*. Edited by R. Scott Rodin. Colbert: Kingdom Life Publishers, 2015.

Ross, Cathy. "Introduction: *Taonga*." In *Mission in the 21st Century: Exploring the Five Marks of Global Mission*. Edited by Andrew Walls and Cathy Ross. Maryknoll: Orbis Books, 2008.

Ross, Cathy. "The Theology of Partnership." *International Bulletin of Missionary Research* 34, no. 3 (2010): 145–48.

Ross, Kenneth R. "Understanding Mission Today: Points of Convergence?", *Transformation* 34, no. 4 (2017).

Roy, Kevin. "South Africa." In *Evangelical Dictionary of World Missions*. Edited by Scott Moreau. Grand Rapids: Baker Books, 2000.

Senior, Donald. "Correlating Images of Church and Images of Mission in the New Testament." *Missiology: An International Review* 13, no. 1 (1995).

Shenk, Wilbert. "Henry Venn." In *Biographical Dictionary of Christian Missions*. Edited by G. Anderson. Grand Rapids: Wm B. Eerdmans, 1998.

Shreve, Kenneth. *Partnership Theology in Creative Access Regions*. Carlisle: Langham Global Library, 2017.

Simon, Mark A. *Living to the Praise of God's Glory: A Missional Reading of Ephesians*. Eugene: Wipf & Stock, 2021.

Skreslet, Stanley. *Comprehending Mission: The Questions, Methods, Themes, Problems and Prospects of Missiology*. Maryknoll: Orbis Books, 2012.

Smith, David. *Mission After Christendom*. London: Darton, Longman and Todd Ltd, 2003.

Smither, Edward. *Christian Mission: A Concise Global History*. Bellingham: Lexham Press, 2019.

Sonea, Cristian. "*Missio Dei* – the Contemporary Missionary Paradigm and its Reception in the Eastern Orthodox Missionary Theology." *Review of*

Ecumenical Studies 9, no. 1 (2017). https://dx.doi.org/10.1515/ress-2017-0006.

Stanley, Brian. *Christianity in the Twentieth Century: A World History*. Princeton: Princeton University Press, 2018.

Stanley, Brian. *The World Missionary Conference, Edinburgh 1910*. Grand Rapids: Wm B. Eerdmans, 2009.

Stark, Rodney. *The Rise of Christianity: A Sociologist Reconsiders History*. Princeton: Princeton University Press, 1996.

Steele, David. *Bold Reformer: Celebrating the Gospel-Centred Convictions of Martin Luther*. Houston: Lucid Books, 2016. Kindle edition.

Stetzer, Ed, and Phil Nation. *The Mission of God: Essays and Letters*. Nashville: LifeWay Press, 2015.

Storti, Craig. *Figuring Foreigners Out: A Practical Guide*. Yarmouth: InterCultural Press, 1999.

Stroope, Michael. *Transcending Mission: The Eclipse of a Modern Tradition*. London: Apollos, 2017.

Sunquist, Scott. *The Unexpected Christian Century*. Grand Rapids: Baker Academic, 2015.

Svelmoe, William. *A New Vision for Missions*. Tuscaloosa: University of Alabama Press, 2008.

Tallman, J. Ray. "Egypt." In *Evangelical Dictionary of World Missions*. Edited by A. Scott Moreau. Grand Rapids: Baker Books, 2000.

Tennent, Timothy. *Invitation to World Missions: A Trinitarian Missiology of the Twenty-First Century*. Grand Rapids: Kregel Academic & Professional, 2010.

Terry, John Mark, and Robert Gallagher. *Encountering the History of Missions: From the Early Church to Today*. Grand Rapids: Baker Academic, 2017.

Terry, John Mark, Ebbie Smith, and Justice Anderson. *Missiology: An Introduction to the Foundations, History, and Strategies of World Missions*. Nashville: Broadman & Holman Publishers, 1998.

Thacker, J. "'The Whole Church': Statement of the Lausanne Theology Working Group." *Evangelical Review of Theology* 34, no. 1 (2010): 4–13.

Tippett, Alan. *Introduction to Missiology*. Pasadena: William Carey Library, 1987.

Tizon, Al. *Transformation After Lausanne: Radical Evangelical Mission in Global-Local Perspective*. Oxford: Regnum Books, 2008.

Tucker, Ruth. *From Jerusalem to Irian Jaya: A Biographical History of Christian Missions*. 2nd ed. Grand Rapids: Zondervan, 2004.

Tyra, Gary. *A Missional Orthodoxy: Theology and Ministry in a Post-Christian Context*. Downers Grove: IVP Academic, 2013.

United Nations. *Urbanisation: Mega & Meta Cities, New City States*. New York: United Nations, 2006.

van Butselaar, G. Jan. "The Role of Churches in the Peace Process in Africa." In *The Changing Face of Christianity: Africa, the West, and the World*.

Edited by Lamin Sanneh and Joel Carpenter. Oxford: Oxford University Press, 2005.

Van Engen, Charles. *Transforming Mission Theology*. Pasadena: William Carey Library, 2017.

Van Wynen, Susan, Dave Crough, and Kirk Franklin. "Foundational Statements of the Wycliffe Global Alliance." 2019. Accessed 7 September, 2020. https://www.wycliffe.net/wp-content/uploads/2020/01/Alliance_Foundational_Statements_2019_09_EN.pdf.

Verkuyl, Johannes. *Contemporary Missiology: An Introduction*. Grand Rapids: Wm B. Eerdmans, 1978.

Walls, Andrew. "Afterword: Christian Mission in a Five-Hundred-Year Context." In *Mission in the 21st Century*. Edited by Andrew Walls and Cathy Ross. Maryknoll: Orbis Books, 2008.

Walls, Andrew. *The Cross-Cultural Process in Christian History*. Maryknoll: Orbis Books, 2017.

Walls, Andrew. "Demographics, Power and the Gospel in the 21st Century." Paper presented to SIL International Conference and WBTI Convention, Waxhaw NC, US, 2002.

Walls, Andrew. *The Missionary Movement in Christian History: Studies in the Transmission of Faith*. Maryknoll: Orbis Books, 1996.

Wan, Enoch. "The Trinitarian Nature of the Mission of God." In *The Mission of God: Essays and Letters*. Edited by Ed Stetzer and Phil Nation. Nashville: LifeWay Press, 2015.

Wan, Enoch, and Kevin Penman. "The 'Why,' 'How' and 'Who' of Partnership in Christian Missions." *Global Missiology* (April 2010).

Whitfield, Keith. "The Triune God: The God of Mission." In *Theology and Practice of Mission: God, the Church, and the Nations*. Edited by Bruce R. Ashford. Nashville: B. & H. Publishing Group, 2011.

Wild-Wood, Emma, and Peniel Rajkumar. *Foundations for Mission*. Oxford: Regnum, 2013.

Wolterstorff, Nicholas. "Foreword." In *Evangelicals and Empire: Christian Alternatives to the Political Status Quo*. Edited by Bruce Benson and Peter Heltzel. Grand Rapids: Brazos Press, 2008.

Woodberry, Robert D. "The Missionary Roots of Liberal Democracy." *American Political Science Review* 106, no. 2 (2012). https://dx.doi.org/10.1017/S0003055412000093.

Wright, Christopher. *The Mission of God: Unlocking the Bible's Grand Narrative*. Downers Grove: IVP Academic, 2006.

Wright, Christopher. *The Mission of God's People*. Grand Rapids: Zondervan, 2010.

Wrogemann, Henning. *Theologies of Mission*. Translated by Karl E. Bohmer. *Intercultural Theology Vol. 2*. Downers Grove: IVP Academic, 2018.

Yeh, Allen. *Polycentric Missiology: Twenty-First Century Mission from Everyone to Everywhere*. Downers Grove: IVP Academic, 2016.

Yong, Amos. *Beyond the Impasse: Toward a Pneumatological Theology of Religions*. Grand Rapids: Baker Academic, 2003.

Zilonka, Paul and Michael Gorman. "The Bible: A Book, a Library, a Story, an Invitation." In *Scripture and Its Interpretation*. Edited by Michael Gorman. Grand Rapids: Baker Academic, 2017, Kindle edition.

Zorgdrager, Heleen. "Moral Guardian or Kenotic Servant? A Theological View of the Role of Churches in Empowering Civil Society in Ukraine." *Occasional Papers on Religion in Eastern Europe* 32, no. 4 (2012): 25–32.

Zurlo, Gina. *Global Christianity: A Guide to the World's Largest Religion From Afghanistan to Zimbabwe*. Grand Rapids: Zondervan Academic, 2022.

Index of Topics and Names